Predictions for America's New War

When Nostradamus wrote his prophecies over four hundred years ago, he could have been burned at the stake for predicting the future. Intentionally cryptic, his quatrains may seem meaningless to readers unfamiliar with European history. This book clearly explains the predictions relating to a Third World War starting in 2002.

Author David Montaigne presents evidence of the accuracy of Nostradamus's predictions of past world events, and takes a serious look at those predictions pertaining to what is happening now and in the future. He takes us through the relevant quatrains, explaining their meaning word by word. In addition, he offers resources to verify the accuracy of the predictions, with web site and book suggestions. He also explains a web hoax dealing with Nostradamus and the World Trade Center, and points to quatrains penned by Nostradamus that are far more alarming.

When will the Third World War or Armageddon actually begin? Montaigne shows us the quatrain describing the fifty-seven years of peace that have come to pass since the end of World War II and the beginning of a new holy war, the likes of which have not been seen since the Great Crusades of the Middle Ages.

Although the message may be one we would rather not hear, Montaigne believes we can avoid catastrophe if we heed Nostradamus's prophetic words.

About the Author

David Montaigne is an entrepreneur by trade, educated as an historian; writing about unusual historical topics is where his true passion lies. His university thesis on Spain's role in World War II was researched in Washington, London, and Madrid—and the same passion for accurate information has gone into producing this book. Introduced to the prophecies of Nostradamus through a movie he watched as a child, he pursued this interest through extensive reading, eventually deciding to write on the subject.

To Write to the Author

If you wish to contact the author or would like more information about this book, please write to the author in care of Llewellyn Worldwide and we will forward your request. Both the author and publisher appreciate hearing from you and learning of your enjoyment of this book and how it has helped you. Llewellyn Worldwide cannot guarantee that every letter written to the author can be answered, but all will be forwarded. Write to:

David S. Montaigne
℅ Llewellyn Worldwide
P.O. Box 64383, Dept. 0-7387-0269-2
St. Paul, MN 55164-0383, U.S.A.

Please enclose a self-addressed stamped envelope for reply, or $1.00 to cover costs. If outside U.S.A., enclose international postal reply coupon.

Many of Llewellyn's authors have websites with additional information and resources. For more information, please visit our website at http://www.llewellyn.com.

NOSTRADAMUS
WORLD WAR III
2002

DAVID S. MONTAIGNE

2002
Llewellyn Publications
St. Paul, Minnesota 55164-0383, U.S.A.

FIRST EDITION
First Printing, 2002

Book interior design and editing by Connie Hill
Cover design by Gavin Dayton Duffy
Cover image © Digital Stock Professional and © Comstock

Library of Congress Cataloging-in-Publication Data
(pending)

Llewellyn Worldwide does not participate in, endorse, or have any authority or responsibility concerning private business transactions between our authors and the public.

All mail addressed to the author is forwarded but the publisher cannot, unless specifically instructed by the author, give out an address or phone number.

Any Internet references contained in this work are current at publication time, but the publisher cannot guarantee that a specific location will continue to be maintained. Please refer to the publisher's website for links to authors' websites and other sources.

Llewellyn Publications
A Division of Llewellyn Worldwide, Ltd.
P.O. Box 64383, Dept. 0-7387-0269-2
St. Paul, MN 55164-0383, U.S.A.
www.llewellyn.com

Printed in the United States of America

From the sky will come
the great King of Terror . . .

Contents

Acknowledgments

I would like to acknowledge the help of Jeffrey Diamond, Sven and Carmen Bilen, Hugh Montaigne, Carl Landgraf, Jim Klein, and many others whose comments have helped shape the final version of this book.

Preface

There are many books about Nostradamus and his prophecies, and you may be trying to decide if this one is any better than the others. The main difference is that this book thoroughly covers a specific amount of relevant material instead of analyzing everything Nostradamus wrote. The book focuses on and clearly explains the prophecies pointing to a Third World War starting in 2002.

This book is also unique for its accuracy. Some authors distort Nostradamus' words, rearranging sentences and even the letters within words to sensationalize the material and create links to current events. As a result there are books entirely devoted to the fabrications and mistakes in some of the popular books on Nostradamus, among them *The Mask of Nostradamus* by James Randi.[1] This author suggests that readers do not take translations and interpretations for granted, and invites readers to verify the material in this book (and to better understand the flaws in other popular

---

1 James Randi. *The Mask of Nostradamus* (Charles Scribner's Sons, New York, 1990).

books) through several excellent sources listed in the bibliography.

I want you to take Nostradamus seriously, but not for the wrong reasons. There are prophecies that many claim describe the events of September 11, 2001, in New York. These are among the many prophecies that have made Nostradamus a household name, but this book will explain why they are not about New York. There are far more impressive successes that should convince even the most doubtful skeptics that Nostradamus did foresee future events, including one describing in amazing detail the fall of the Soviet Union and the end of the Cold War. Unfortunately, Nostradamus' version of history has proven to be accurate right up to the new millenium, and we must take very seriously his prediction of a Third World War starting in 2002.

♦ ♦ ♦

Supposed New York Prophecies

Quatrain 10:72

The year 1999, seventh month,
From the sky will come the great King
*   of Terror:*
To revive the great king of the Angolmois,
Before and after Mars reigns by good luck.

This may be Nostradamus' most famous quatrain—but only because of the mention of the year 1999 and gross misinterpretation. There isn't any link to New York in this quatrain, but some authors connect it to other quatrains that mention a new city. Fortunately those who expected nuclear bombs falling on New York to be the great King of Terror in 1999 were wrong.

Basic Interpretation: The great eclipse of 1999 will mark the beginning of Chinese expansion and militarism.

Detailed Interpretation: A total eclipse of the sun is a rare event, only possible in the same location every 360 years. In Nostradamus' day people were more superstitious, and the fates of kings and empires were believed to be foretold by omens. The most impressive omens were unusual events in the sky, such as comets and eclipses— "From the sky will come the great King of Terror." On August 11, 1999, a full solar eclipse was seen over Europe and the Middle East. Considering the modern changes in our calendar to correct for old inaccuracies, it would have been late in the seventh month of July in Nostradamus' old calendar—"The year 1999, seventh month." Complete darkness at mid-day caused by the unusual disappearance of the sun was a major King of Terror in the sky.

The "King of the Angolmois" is an anagram for "Mongolias." In times past Genghis Khan was a great king of terror, spreading the Mongol horde across Asia and ruling the largest empire ever known. Just months after the eclipse the tomb of Genghis Khan was found in China's northwestern province of Xinjiang, a mostly Muslim region near Afghanistan.[2] The symbolic links between this vast Asian empire, modern-day China, Muslims, conquest and terror, and the time of the eclipse seem too significant for mere coincidence. Nostradamus probably means that the army of China, Mongolia's cultural brother and heir to the legacy (and body) of Genghis Khan—will be reawakened

---

2 John Schauble. "Claim on Genghis Khan tomb sure to rile Mongolia" (*Sydney Morning Herald*, 9/18/2000).

soon after this marker in time—"To bring back to life the great king of the Angolmois."

China did regain Hong Kong in 1999, and further Chinese expansion seems likely. Many Chinese resent America's protection of Taiwan, the rebel Chinese province they have not yet united with mainland China, and Taiwan will be ripe for the picking if America's greatly reduced military is kept too busy in Afghanistan, Iraq, or other Islamic nations. It seems likely that China will take advantage of America's preoccupation with the Islamic world and start to gain territory in Asia. This window of opportunity may be the explanation of the last line about war (Mars) being linked to the good fortune of America being too busy to intervene—"Before and after Mars reigns by good luck."

Do not take the prophecy for 1999 lightly just because nothing sensational happened then like the nuclear destruction of New York. Nostradamus has a thousand prophecies, but mentions specific years only twelve times. 1999 is the only date he gives between the French Revolution in 1792 and the end of the world in 3797, and he attributes great significance to the events following the eclipse of 1999.

Two other quatrains are often interpreted to describe a supposed nuclear attack in 1999—but there are better explanations for these two verses that do not involve nuclear weapons.

Quatrain 10:49

Garden of the world near the new city,
In the way of the hollow mountains:
It will be seized and plunged into the Tub,
Forced to drink waters by sulfur poisoned.

Many sources said that New York is the new city in the new world, near the Garden State of New Jersey. The path of the hollow mountains could be the eastern seaboard of cities, with skyscrapers from Virginia to Massachusetts. The last two lines suggest it would be destroyed and plunged into the polluted sea.

Although that interpretation is not too far-fetched, there is a more likely one. The city of Naples is in the very fertile Campaignia region of southern Italy. Naples is Italian for the original Greek name Neopolis. *Neo* means new, *polis* means city. "Garden of the world near the new city." The area around Naples is a very fertile garden because of all the mineral-rich volcanic ash from nearby Mt. Vesuvius, a hollow mountain that occasionally spews sulfurous lava that flows in a path through the valley Naples is in—"In the way of the hollow mountains." Naples is on the coast and lava would simply melt, burn, and carry whatever was left of the city into the Mediterranean—"It will be seized and plunged into the Tub, Forced to drink waters poisoned by sulfur"—if Mt. Vesuvius does have a major eruption. Although this could happen in any year, Italian earthquakes and volcanic eruptions have become increasingly common these last few years, and they are a sign that Edgar Cayce[3] indicated would precede World War III.

This analysis is supported by quatrain 1:87:

> *Volcanic fire from the center of the earth*
> *Will make trembling around the new city:*
> *Two great rocks for a long time shall make*
> *   war.*
> *Then Arethusa will make a new red river.*

There are no volcanoes near New York. This clearly describes "volcanic" activity and a "red river" of lava near the "new city," (neo polis) which is Naples, Italy. Naples is twelve miles from Mt. Vesuvius, closer than Pompeii was. "Arethusa" is a mythical figure who chased a man to Syracuse, a town in Sicily. Perhaps the lava and ash will chase away the inhabitants of Naples. Both Syracuse and Naples are in southern Italy. This will occur when "two great rocks" are making war for a long time. Islam and Christianity in World War III?

Another quatrain somehow associated with the nuclear destruction of New York is 6:97:

> *At forty-five degrees the sky will burn,*
> *Fire to approach the great new city:*
> *Instantly a great scattered flame will leap up,*
> *When they shall make a trial of the Normans.*

---

3 Edgar Cayce is a famous American psychic, most noted for his abilities to heal the sick, but he also made many predictions of future events, including several about World War III.

If New York were closer to 45 degrees north (instead of 40.75) there would be less reason to doubt the popular, sensational meaning that New York is "the great new city." But another Nostradamus scholar, Rolfe Boswell (*Nostradamus Speaks*, 1941), noted that Halifax, Canada's main naval base, was of course not yet established in Nostradamus' day but is also a new city, in the new world, and is almost exactly "At forty-five degrees" latitude. There was a large explosion there on October 6, 1917, resulting in a huge fire—"the sky will burn, fire to approach the great new city"—and numerous deaths. This occurred at the peak of World War I, and sabotage was suspected—"Instantly a great scattered flame will leap up"—the prime suspects being the crew of a Norwegian ship—"they shall make a trial of the Normans." Norway is the homeland of the Norman invaders who settled in northern France.

The last prophecy very accurately and successfully predicted an event—but it has happened already, in Halifax in 1917. It does not describe the destruction of New York, although many authors like to force such interpretations. Consider a recent example that was e-mailed repeatedly just after the terrorism of September 11, 2001:

> *In the City of God there will be a great*
> *   thunder,*
> *Two brothers torn apart by Chaos,*
> *while the fortress endures,*
> *the great leader will succumb,*

> *The third big war will begin when the*
>   *big city is burning.*

Nostradamus 1654

Some would say this is a prophecy regarding the destruction of the Twin Towers, but it's an obvious hoax. Nostradamus died in 1566. Not only did he not write the material attributed to him above, he never wrote in that style. His prophecies are written in four-line quatrains, not five lines. He never mentioned a "City of God" (would that really describe New York anyway?) or "the third big war." This hoax started with a university student who invented it in an essay on Nostradamus to show how an impressive-sounding prophecy can be made with the use of vague wording, but his material made it to a web page, and was taken seriously by some despite the main point of the essay. Since September 11, 2001, more lines have been added to the original made-up version:

> *On the 11th day of the 9th month,*
> *two metal birds will crash into two tall statues*
> *in the new city,*
> *and the world will end soon after.*

This alleged prophecy is just one recent example of an attempt to sensationalize Nostradamus and force a clear link to current events. Sadly, far more successful authors have sunk just as low. It is so common for authors to abuse Nostradamus in this way that James Randi has written an entire book exposing the authors.[4] Yet the more they warp and sensationalize the material, the more successful their books are. Movies have been even more "inaccurate and exaggerated and distorted" but have had at least twenty times the impact on American knowledge of Nostradamus than the books that came before them.[5]

Popular interest in Nostradamus is based almost entirely on falsified and sensationalized information, and if you already believed that Nostradamus could see the future based on other sources then you were probably convinced by these deceptions. In many books the author will mix and match sentences from different prophecies and present the end result as if he or she and Nostradamus had written them together. Sometimes they don't even keep the lines intact, but will rearrange individual words, and on occasion, even the letters in the words will be changed.[6] Many readers have taken these alterations seriously, and have been convinced that Nostradamus was right—for all the wrong reasons.

---

4 Taking great poetic license to alter Nostradamus' prophecies is not a modern phenomenon. Many seventeenth-century editors routinely did whatever was necessary to make the quatrains rhyme in English, including rearranging the lines and adding words. One example is William Atwood's *Wonderful Predictions of Nostradamus, Grebner, David Pareus, and Antonius Torquatus* (J. Robinson, London, 1689).

5 Edgar Leoni. *Nostradamus and His Prophecies* (Bell Publishing, New York, 1982), p. 72.

6 There are a few "nonsense" words with no inherent meaning, like "Zopyra" and "Angolmois" that are anagrams Nostradamus intended interpreters to understand, but many authors will take perfectly good French words and warp them.

It doesn't have to be that way! Nostradamus made some amazingly accurate predictions of future events, and it isn't necessary to change a single word to lead to these interpretations. How will you know the difference, you ask? How will you know that the interpretations are right?

You could simply wait out the end of 2002. Another way to verify these interpretations requires old-fashioned R&D. Research. Contact Jacqueline Allemand, who runs the Nostradamus museum in Salon-de-Provence, France. She will be happy to point out absurd distortions of Nostradamus' writings in modern publications. Get a book containing Nostradamus' original writings in medieval French.[7] I highly recommend Edgar Leoni's *Nostradamus and His Prophecies* as an objective reference tool; it gives the original French version on the left pages and English on the right, with no personal interpretations or speculative rewording.[8] Get a French-English dictionary and a book on the history of Western civilization, or use the encyclopedia on your computer. Then you can verify every quotation and every interpretation in this book for linguistic and historical accuracy.

Even better, start with James Randi's *The Mask of Nostradamus*; especially the chapter that is entirely devoted

---

7 I was fortunate to have access to very old sources such as Garencieres' *The True Prophecies or Prognostications of Michael Nostradamus* (1672), but also recommend the more easily accessible and excellent *Nostradamus and His Prophecies* by Edgar Leoni (1982).

8 Leoni, ibid.

to disproving the "ten pieces of the evidence most used to prove that Nostradamus had prophetic ability."[9] None of them are clear successes, but many other predictions are.

◆ ◆ ◆

9 Randi, ibid.

2

Nostradamus' Most Successful Prophecy

This is probably the single most successful prophecy so far. It is a long one, but it is accurate down to the fine details. The lines below are a section from paragraphs 25 and 26 of a letter Nostradamus wrote in 1558 to King Henry II of Navarre:

> . . . reversals of realms and great earthquakes, along with the procreation of the new Babylon, miserable daughter increased by the abomination of the first holocaust, and it will last for only seventy-three years and seven months. Afterwards to come forth from the stock which had remained barren for so long, proceeding from the 50th degree, one

who will renew the whole Christian Church.
There will be a pinnacle of great peace, with
union and concord between some of the chil-
dren of opposite ideas and separated by
diverse realms. And such will be the peace that
chained to the deepest pit of hell will remain
the instigator and promoter of military
factions. And the kingdom of the Furious One,
who counterfeits the sage, will be united.

Basic Interpretation: These paragraphs clearly describe the collapse of the Soviet Union in 1991.

Detailed Interpretation: "Great earthquakes" were hitting cities in California, Japan, Mexico, and Italy near the beginning of the 1990s. Kuwait was conquered by Iraq in 1990, then was liberated in 1991 and Iraq surrendered. Germany reunited and then the Soviet Union fell apart— "reversals of realms."

Babylon was known for its many subject peoples with their different languages, which led to the story of the Tower of Babel. The Soviet Union, with its domination over Finns, Estonians, Latvians, Lithuanians, Poles, Germans, Ukrainians, Moldavians, Georgians, Armenians, Kazakhs, Uzbeks, Tajiks, and many others, easily fits the description as a new Babylon in this comparison. The Soviet Union was also called the Evil Empire (at least by Ronald Reagan), and Babylon is one of the Bible's prime examples of an evil empire.

The Soviet Union did "procreate" in 1991; it broke apart, giving birth to many independent nations. The Soviet Union was a daughter: the offspring of Mother Russia. It was miserable enough that every single republic wanted independence from Russian domination. It was increased in two ways: it emerged from World War II as one of the main superpowers, and it was the only nation enlarged by "the first holocaust" of World War II. All the other major powers kept their borders or lost territory, but the Soviet Union expanded west into Europe and east into Manchuria.

Most impressive of all, the Soviet Union lasted for "seventy-three years and seven months." On January 18, 1918, Lenin's Bolsheviks shut down the democratically elected government of Russia and began the seizure of power. On August 18, 1991, a KGB-led coup took Mikhail Gorbachev hostage and demanded his resignation. His government's weakness allowed every non-Russian republic to secede and declare independence.[10]

Poland is "the stock which had remained barren for so long"—it had not produced a great leader in centuries; it had been barren stock. But Pope John Paul II has invigorated the Church and governed it during great modernization and adaptations to technological and

---

10 In both cases, there was turmoil for a few months. It took several months in early 1918 for the Bolsheviks to consolidate their control over Russia's rural areas or execute the czar. And although several former Soviet republics declared independence in August 1991, others took longer to react to the weakness and chaos of the Soviet Union's death throes. It was not until December 1991 that Russian leaders formally admitted that the Soviet Union no longer existed.

social changes. He was also instrumental in freeing Poland from the Soviets and in organizing missionary work in Russia, effectively welcoming half of Europe back to Christianity after generations of enforced atheism. He did much to "renew the whole Christian Church." John Paul II is also from Krakow, a city at the 50th degree north latitude. All other popes in the last few centuries have been from Italy—too far south.

The end of the cold war came between the ideologically opposite superpowers—"great peace will be established, with union and concord between some of the children of opposite ideas." The last line says that "the kingdom of the Furious One, who counterfeits the sage, will be united." Adolf Hitler[11] behaved in a rather rabid and furious fashion, and he did believe that God was helping him. The Germans accepted him as a virtual messiah. Germany was reunited in late 1990, less than a year before these events.

Coincidence? Many who doubt Nostradamus' prophetic ability note that anyone could make up a thousand vague predictions, and that after a few centuries there are sure to be some apparently marvelous successes. But is seventy-three years and seven months vague? Do those lines seem like a coincidence to you? If you didn't already take Nostradamus seriously, maybe such a successful prophecy has convinced you. And in case one success is not enough, there are many more.

---

11 Nostradamus does not refer to Hitler as an antichrist, although other authors identify Napoleon and Hitler as two antichrists.

3

Other Successful Prophecies

Quatrain 4:54

Of a name never had by a Gallic King
Never was there a thunderbolt so fearful,
Trembling Italy, Spain, and the English,
To foreign women much attention.

Basic Interpretation: Napoleon.

Detailed Interpretation: Gaul was the name for France in Roman times, and "Gallic" means French. No French *king* was ever named Napoleon, but that is because Napoleon was an emperor, not a king. Nostradamus often employs this kind of wordplay. Napoleon led an army larger than any other in the history of the world up to that time, across Europe, conquering nations all the way to Moscow. The Grand Armee was truly a fearful thunderbolt of war. Napoleon conquered Italy and Spain completely, and made his brothers kings in those countries. The English were the only rivals that he had not invaded, but they feared invasion. They abandoned their war against the United States, the War of 1812, even though they were winning, and had already burned Washington, D.C., to the ground. To the British, a weak American enemy across thousands of miles of ocean was far less important than a strong enemy only a few miles across the English Channel. The trembling British gave Napoleon top priority and rushed back to Europe to fight him. Lastly, Napoleon's love life was full of foreign women. His first wife, Josephine, was a Creole. His second wife, Marie Louise, was from Austria. His mistress, Marie Walewska, was Polish.

Quatrain 5:4

The large mastiff expelled from the city
Will be angered by the strange alliance,
After chasing the stag to the fields,
The wolf and the bear will defy each other.

Basic Interpretation: France surrenders in World War II, Churchill is vexed, Germany and Russia soon fight.

Detailed Interpretation: A mastiff is a dog, and Britain was famous for its mastiffs.[12] Winston Churchill was known as the British Bulldog. In June 1940 he watched

---

12 Garencieres, ibid., p. 195.

the French army collapse and tried to rally them on until he was expelled from the city by the German advance into Paris just four days later. When the French prophet says "the city" he generally means Paris. Churchill was angered that Russia, France's traditional ally against Germany, did nothing. The nonaggression pact between Hitler and Stalin was certainly a "strange alliance" and is often referred to as an unholy one. Racist German fascism was diametrically opposed to the ideological universal brotherhood of Soviet Communism. The Polish flag once had a deer (stag) on it. Russia and Germany invaded Poland together and then waited almost two years to fight each other afterward. The bear is associated with Russia just as the eagle is with America. Hitler identified strongly with wolves, naming the majority of his command posts Werewolf, Wolf's Lair, and Wolf's Ravine. He even loved to whistle the Disney tune, "Who's Afraid of the Big Bad Wolf?"

Quatrain 2:9

Nine years reigns the gaunt one in peaceful land,
Then to fall into a bloody thirst:
Because of him a great people without faith and law die
Slaughtered by one much more good-natured.

Basic Interpretation: Franklin Delano Roosevelt doesn't stop the extermination of the Jews in World War II.

Detailed Interpretation: FDR was crippled by polio and years in a wheelchair left many muscles emaciated and gaunt. He led America, "a peaceful land," and the United States stayed neutral at the start of World War II until "nine years" after his election to the presidency. He ruled for nine years of peace, then ruled in war. American forces then spread around the world aggressively, despite great bloodshed. FDR was aware of the holocaust but vetoed various actions that could have saved many Jews, opting for total military victory in Europe as the best way to end human suffering altogether. This was a tough decision made when the Allies were losing and America had to focus on military victory. Hitler was winning and could spare thousands of men from the front lines to round up the Jews, thus most of the Jewish race died horribly, unprotected by laws and losing faith that they were God's chosen people. The Jews were slaughtered under Hitler's orders, and while Hitler was evil, and suicidal by the end of the war, he had great personal charisma. He was filmed doing a little victory dance when France surrendered, and in those early days of German victories he was the good-natured whistler of tunes.

Quatrain 4:56

After the victory of the raving tongue,
The spirit tempered in tranquility and
*   repose:*
The bloody victor through the conflict makes
*   orations,*
Roasting the tongue and the flesh and the
*   bones.*

Basic Interpretation: The vicious, yet good-natured Hitler burns the Jews in the Holocaust.

Detailed Interpretation: Hitler came to power largely because he was such a powerful speaker. But in victory Hitler was tranquil and calm, not troubled at all by his evil crimes against humanity. He had great faith he was right and that fate would lead him to victory. Meanwhile his "final solution" for the Jews was to burn them in ovens.

Quatrain 3:88

From Barcelona by sea a great army,
All Marseilles with terror will tremble:
Isles seized help shut off by sea,
Your traitor on land will swim.

Basic Interpretation: Spain attacked Marseilles and failed even with a traitor in the city.

Detailed Interpretation: The interpretation of this one is agreed upon by most Nostradamus scholars. In 1596 Philip II of Spain was at war with France and he wanted to capture the port of Marseilles. To help his forces on land defeat the defenders of Marseilles, his navy left Barcelona and surrounded Marseilles' coast. The Spanish took over the small islands in the bay to help block any enemy ships attempting to aid the French—"Isles seized help shut off by sea." Charles de Casau had attempted to betray Marseilles and aid the Spanish efforts to take his city. The offensive failed, however, and his French countrymen killed him and dragged the corpse of this traitor through the gutters of the muddy streets, a means of swimming on land.

Quatrain 4:96

The elder sister of the British Isle
Fifteen years before her brother will be born,
Because of her promise in return for
verification,
She will succeed to the reign of the balance.

Basic Interpretation: The American democracy is born fifteen years before the French.

Detailed Interpretation: In 1215 the Magna Carta first brought democracy to Britain. The next democracy was born in the United States in 1776. America is the elder of Britain's siblings. Fifteen years later, in 1791, the French Republic was born as the monarchy was overthrown and the French Revolution began. The French democracy is America's brother. The promise may be the rights of free men established in the Constitution and Bill of Rights. Verification may refer to French support and eventual independence as a sovereign nation. For centuries Britain maintained the role of the balance, making sure no aggressor grew too powerful in Europe, and siding against the dominant nation whenever France or Germany or Russia became too powerful. Eventually the British Empire grew weak and America took over this role as protector of the weak, defender against the strong.

Quatrain 2:68

The efforts of Aquilon will be great:
The window on the ocean will be opened,
The kingdom on the isle will be restored:
London will tremble by sails discovered.

Basic Interpretation: Russia founds St. Petersburg after the British monarchy is restored to power.

Detailed Interpretation: Aquilon is the mythical land of the north wind; Nostradamus means Russia. In the late seventeenth century Russia was landlocked and warred with Sweden in order to gain some waterfront property on the Baltic Sea. Temporary gains were surrendered back to Sweden in 1661. The Russians' efforts were great, however; they did not give up. Peter the Great came to power, and he believed that Russia would not be a first class power unless it had a navy to defend its interests. To have a navy, he would need at least one seaport—and Russia would have to seize the land from Sweden. Once he finally captured a suitable coastal site, Peter moved the capital from Moscow to what he referred to as his "window on the sea." St. Petersburg was eventually founded there in 1703.

The late seventeenth century also saw "the kingdom on the isle restored" when the English military dictator Cromwell died in 1660 and Charles II was crowned king. This happened just before the Russian efforts to start a seaport in the Baltic, which lasted from about 1660 to the end of the war with Sweden in 1721. Lastly the Dutch navy did sail up the Thames River and raid the London area in 1667. In 1669 the same navy brought William of Orange to seize London's monarchy from Charles' successor, James II. This quatrain is especially important because Peter's window shows beyond a doubt that Aquilon is Russia, and not some other northern land such as England, which is directly north of Nostradamus' French homeland. Many other quatrains mentioning Aquilon would have little meaning without this insight.

Quatrain 1:70

Rain, famine, war in Persia not ceasing,
The too great faith shall betray the monarch,
Finished there commenced in Gaul:
Secret omen for one to be moderate.

Basic Interpretation: In 1979 the Shah of Iran was overthrown by Islamic fundamentalists.

Detailed Interpretation: Gaul was the Roman name for France, and if Nostradamus was randomly guessing that a conspiracy in France would overthrow a monarch thousands of miles away in Persia (now Iran) he was really going out on a limb. We are used to nations extending their influence around the world, but in 1555 France had little impact on Persian politics. In 1979, however, disasters, including floods and food shortages—rain and famine—were devastating Iran. Such conditions cause public unrest, and have been the cause of many revolutions. In this case Islamic fundamentalists—"the too great faith"—overthrew the monarch, the Shah of Iran. The leader of this religious movement, the Ayatollah Khomeni, had been exiled years earlier by the Shah, and had organized the revolution in Paris. The sign "for one to be moderate" probably refers to another monarch in the Muslim world. Perhaps fear of being overthrown by the religious fundamentalist elements of society had an impact on the royal family of Saudi Arabia. Their king could have the same fate as Iran's Shah if they ignore the threat of "the too great faith."

Quatrain 5:85

Through the Swiss and neighboring places,
They will be at war over the clouds:
Swarm of marine locusts and mosquitoes,
The faults of Geneva shall be laid quite bare.

Basic Interpretation: Aerial combat near Switzerland, through the fault of the Swiss in Geneva.

Detailed Interpretation: France, Germany, and Italy surround Switzerland, and all three were involved in aerial combat—"war over the clouds"—in World War II. Eventually British and American forces dominated the seas and skies of Europe, and this swarm of Allied ships and planes all came from across the sea, either the Atlantic or the English Channel. "Locusts and mosquitoes" probably refer to ships and planes. The war came about because there was no real power invested in the League of Nations, which was centered in Geneva. It could do little more than protest aggression and watch the spread of war. Kudos to Nostradamus, especially for understanding aerial warfare at a point in history when it would have been incomprehensible to most.

The weakness of Geneva's League of Nations is also described in quatrain 1:47:

> *From the Lake of Geneva the sermons*
> *annoying,*
> *From days they will grow into weeks,*
> *Then months, then years, then all will fail,*
> *The Magistrates will damn their useless laws.*

Basic Interpretation: The League of Nations was powerless, a shell of laws it couldn't enforce.

Detailed Interpretation: The League first condemned Japan in 1931 for its invasion of the Chinese province of

Manchuria. The Japanese soon grew tired of Geneva's lectures and simply canceled their membership in the organization. Any remaining credibility was lost a few years later when nothing was done in response to Italian aggression in Ethiopia. This failure of useless laws led Hitler to realize that other nations would not be inclined to interfere with German expansion, and World War II was the result.

Quatrain 4:15

From where they will think to make the
    famine come,
From there will come the superabundance:
The eye of the sea through canine greed
For the one the other will give oil, wheat.

Basic Interpretation: German submarines almost starved Britain out of World War II.

Detailed Interpretation: In the early years of World War II the Germans hoped that by sinking their supply boats they could starve the British into famine and surrender, but Britain became known as "an unsinkable aircraft carrier" and was eventually the staging area for the invasion of France. By 1944 the Allies had stored up such a superabundance of supplies and troops that the invasion was unstoppable. The Germans had sunk British supply ships using submarines, which operated in canine groups called wolf packs, and targeted their prey through periscopes, "the eye of the sea." Territorial greed led them into war with the British. British shipping losses from submarine warfare never brought England to the point of famine because the island received so many supplies from the United States. America's two main exports to Britain were oil and wheat.

Quatrain 8:15

Towards Aquilon great exertions by the
   manlike woman,
Almost Europe and the World to vex,
The two eclipses she will put to chase,
And to the Pannonians life and death
   reinforced.

Basic Interpretation: Germany almost conquers Russia; Britain, France, Austria, and Hungary suffer too.

Detailed Interpretation: Germany almost conquered Russia, Europe, and the world. As Lady Liberty symbolizes America, the female Germania symbolizes Germany. But she is very masculine in her zest for war. In World War I and World War II German forces extended farthest into Aquilon—Russia. The two eclipses are the two empires of Britain and France, their great power fading away like the light during an eclipse while German forces pounded them almost to total defeat. Both empires have been lost after the two homelands were greatly weakened by wars with Germany. The Pannonias are the Roman province that now comprises Austria and Hungary, which lost World War I as Germany's allies. When Germany again fought Britain, France, and Russia in World War II, Austria and Hungary came close to victory a second time, yet suffered defeat a second time—life and death reinforced—for being on Germany's side.

Quatrain 6:37

The ancient work will be finished,
From the ceiling will fall on the great one
 evil ruin:
Being dead, they will accuse an innocent
 of the deed,
The guilty one hidden in the misty
 brushwood.

Basic Interpretation: Kennedy was assassinated, but Oswald didn't do it.

Detailed Interpretation: This is just a popular theory, and not universally accepted history, but the quatrain fits the theory very well. Assassination is an ancient line of work. Oswald supposedly shot JFK from not far below the roof (the ceiling) of the book depository building in Dallas, and was himself conveniently shot to death within days. Once Oswald (who claimed to be an innocent pawn) was dead, the case was largely closed. If there was a large conspiracy, Oswald was not alive to tell about it, and there were no other official suspects. Decades later, many assume Oswald was a pawn for more powerful conspirators. Some photographs do show a vague outline of a man with a cowboy hat and a rifle lying down in the grassy knoll of bushes in the highway divider in front of Kennedy's motorcade—"The guilty one hidden in the misty brushwood." Roughly fifty eyewitnesses described a shot coming from that area, but when one policeman found a man with a gun there, the man flashed his CIA identification and the officer moved on.

Quatrain 9:16

From Castile Franco will come the assembly,
The ambassador not pleasing will cause a
*   schism:*
Those of Riviera will be in the melee,
And they will refuse entry to the great gulf.

Basic Interpretation: Franco ruled Spain wisely and kept it out of World War II.

Detailed Interpretation: Castile was the largest kingdom in what became Spain. Francisco Franco was the dictator who ruled Spain from 1939 to 1975, and he was from the area once called Castile. He led a rebellion against the Spanish Assembly, the government elected in 1936. The Spanish Civil War lasted from 1936 to 1939, largely because foreign governments interfered, sending just enough military supplies to prevent their side from losing. Rivera was the last right-wing dictator before Franco; and "those of Riviera" could mean the supporters of the Spanish right-wing that followed Franco. But the word Riviera refers to the northwest Mediterranean coast, and most specifically to northwest Italy. The Italians helped Franco's rebel forces and eventually forced the Soviets to stop supplying the legitimate government—by torpedoing Russian ships on the way to Spain. This denied the Soviet navy an entrance to the great gulf of the Mediterranean.

Italy and Germany helped Franco and they wanted Spain to join their side in World War II, but the civil war had left Spain too weak to fight. So that Hitler would not be angry, Franco encouraged his government's foreign minister to act almost as an ambassador to Germany. Franco used him to play good cop, bad cop; Franco stayed silent on what Spain would do and let his right-hand man do all the talking about how Spain would, any day now, join the Germans and Italians in the war. Then Germany invaded Russia, and failed to overwhelm it, and America was fighting Germany as well. When the Allies had the upper hand, Franco could no longer allow his controversial and disagreeable ambassador to keep saying how pro-German Spain was—it angered the powerful nations that were expected to win the war. Franco suddenly fired his "Axis ambassador," causing temporary government turmoil, a schism in the ranks of a largely pro-German government. In late 1942 the Allies landed in North Africa, almost within sight of southern Spain.

The Germans again asked to go through Spain, this time to get to North Africa. Again, Franco refused, denying Hitler the opportunity to cross the Mediterranean, the "great gulf."

This quatrain is a great example because I wouldn't have a clue what Nostradamus meant if I had not done years of research on an obscure and unusual topic—a neutral country's role in a war. Without a historical explanation, that quatrain would be meaningless to most people, but because I happen to be familiar with that bit of history, the quatrain's meaning is instantly recognizable to me, and amazingly detailed and accurate. How many of Nostradamus' prophecies have been accurately fulfilled without most people—or even most historians—recognizing the accomplishment?

♦ ♦ ♦

4

Drawing the Line

The previous quatrains are very clear. Many others seem partially successful, or are too vague to pin down to a specific event. Quatrain 5:79 is a great example of a prophecy with more than one valid interpretation:

> *The sacred pomp will come to lower its*
> *wings,*
> *Through the coming of the great lawgiver:*
> *He will raise the humble, he will vex the*
> *rebels,*
> *His likeness will not appear on this earth.*

Interpretation 1: The Confederacy was very pompous in its belief in slavery. Southerners held the idea of white supremacy so sacred that they were willing to destroy the nation and fight a civil war over it, but the Confederacy had to lower its flag in defeat at the end of America's civil war. Abraham Lincoln was first a lawyer, then a law-maker, as a congressman, and as president he signed the

Emancipation Proclamation, one of the nation's most important laws. He raised the humble slaves to the status of equal citizens, and defeated the rebels. No other president has been so crucial to the successful destiny of the American nation.

Interpretation 2: Napoleon Bonaparte belittled the sacred pomp of the Catholic Church. He arrogantly took the crown out of the pope's hands and crowned himself Emperor of France in 1804. He then forced Francis II to renounce his title as Holy Roman Emperor in 1806, destroying that sacred pomp. The Empire ceased to exist; its wings were permanently lowered. The Napoleonic Code is still the basis of modern French law, making Napoleon France's greatest lawgiver. Napoleon reorganized the social elite, and many low-born peasants were granted nobility, which raised the humble. He butchered his rebellious opposition. No other European leader has come so close to ruling Europe. Hitler tried, but he failed to capture Moscow as Napoleon did.

This quatrain has two possible interpretations. Others are even more vague, remaining more open to interpretation. Many quatrains not covered in this book do refer to World War III—but not with enough clear detail to make use of them. Quatrain 2:21 mentions an ambassador sent overseas in line 1, trouble, binding with ropes and chains, and in line 4 mentions "Negropont." The United States ambassador to the United Nations is John D. Negroponte—but the middle of the quatrain is too obscure to lead me to a clear interpretation of future events. Other quatrains refer to war, but are vague enough to describe several wars. Some prophecies are remarkably accurate but require too much historical explanation to fit in the beginning of this book. Over twenty paragraphs of the letter to King Henry II (already cited for the reference to the fall of the Soviet Union) describe European history from the 1920s to the early twenty-first century in great detail. While an analysis of so much material is not appropriate at this point in the book, readers interested in the bulk of this letter should read the section near the end of this book that covers its successes in detail.

Hundreds of Nostradamus' predictions have come to pass successfully. He accurately described the fall of the Soviet Union and the end of the Cold War in 1991, the eclipse of 1999, and the discovery of Genghis Khan's tomb in 2000. These successes do not seem like mere coincidence, and they demonstrate that the path of history that Nostradamus foresaw in the 1550s is still right on track into the new millennium. This is unfortunate, for he writes of a horrible war that will be under way by 2002. He clearly foresees a war between Christianity and Islam,[13] and even describes an Islamic leader that can only be Osama bin Laden.

---

13 This analysis dates to at least 1656, when Etienne Jaubert intended to expand his writings on Nostradamus and include two volumes devoted to the theme of Christianity vs. Islam and the Antichrist (Leoni, ibid., p. 62).

5

When Does
World War III Begin?

Nostradamus does not organize his prophecies in chrono-logical order; we cannot simply turn to his section on the twenty-first century. His writings are disorganized, vague, and often difficult to interpret. With this in mind, consider this interpretation: that World War III will begin in 2002.

Quatrain 10:89

From brick to marble, the walls will be
  converted,
Seven and fifty peaceful years:
Joy to mankind, the aqueduct renewed,
Health, abundant fruits, joy and honey-
  making times.

Basic Interpretation: Progress for fifty-seven years between World War II and World War III, happy peace-time in France from 1945 to 2002.

Detailed Interpretation: After the devastating bomb-ings of World War II, most of Europe's cities were piles of crumbled bricks. These cities were rebuilt, often with elegant marble—but that word indicates the traditional improvement upon the old, in a hierarchy including straw, sticks, bricks, and marble. The postwar period saw "the aqueduct renewed," a return to the normal flow of progress and trade, technological progress, med-ical advances, modern conveniences, economic prosper-ity, easy availability of food—the highest standard of living humanity has ever known. But there are only fifty-seven years of such peace, so if mid-1945 is the starting point, then 2002 would be the end. France has never seen such a long peace since the time of Nos-tradamus; no previous era fits the description at all.

Quatrain 6:24

Mars and the sceptre are found conjoined
Under Cancer calamitous war:
A little later a new King anointed,
Who for a long time pacifies the earth.

Basic Interpretation: There will be a big war in 2002 and then a great new king will bring peace to the earth.

Detailed Interpretation: Cancer is a sign of the zodiac and a description of the region of the sky with the constellation Cancer in it. At some point in time the planet Mars will appear to come close to "the sceptre" the symbol of supreme authority—which would mean Jupiter, in the hierarchy of Roman gods and modern names for planets. Mars and Jupiter appear next to each other in Cancer, which, according to Dr. Christian Wollner's calculations, happens only on June 21, 2002.[14] Soon after the war begins "a new King" (not king), brings peace to the earth. Nostradamus may mean the second coming of the Christian messiah, as his main themes for World War III are that it is the biblical apocalypse,[15] that in human form three antichrists will lead the Islamic alliance, and that Satan's influence will end with the war, after which God will give mankind a thousand years of peace. But it is also possible that he means England or another European nation will have a new king. Nostradamus often refers to "the King of Europe" that will lead Christianity to victory over Islam.[16]

---

14 Christian Wollner. *The Mystery of Nostradamus* (Berlin, 1926), p. 59.

15 The course of World War III that I foresee allows for all three of the basic themes that Nostradamus' prophecies seem so concerned with. As Leoni described them, they are new Charlemagne . . . the new Arab empire, or that of the removal of the Papacy from "Rome" (Leoni, ibid., p. 110). Charlemagne was the emperor who unified France over a thousand years ago.

16 I am not attempting to foment problems between Christians and Muslims; these are simply the facts. Nostradamus repeatedly described the upcoming war in terms of Christians versus Muslims (or less politically correct terms favored in his time, such as infidels

Paragraph five of Nostradamus' letter to King Henry II relates:

> *. . . at the beginning of the seventh millennary, when so far as my profound computations and astronomical calculations have been able to make out, the adversaries of Jesus Christ and his Church begin to multiply greatly.*

Basic Interpretation: Near the year 2000 the enemies of the Christian world will start to rise up.

Detailed Interpretation: Early Church officials disagreed on the timing of creation, but if we use the most widely accepted year 4004 B.C. for the official beginning of the world, then his reference to "the beginning of the seventh millenary" would mean shortly after 1996. Six millennia had passed since the creation of the world if we assume that 4004 B.C. was the first year.[17] Certainly

---

and barbarians). Muslims have contributed greatly to Western civilization, and my intention is not to diminish their culture or religion with any negative connotations. But Nostradamus is not politically correct, and neither are modern leaders discussing the coming war. Islamic leaders often refer to a jihad, or holy war, against Christian barbarians, and even President Bush has referred to the coming war as a crusade.

17 Although many early chronologies varied between the Byzantine calculation of 5500 B.C. and the beginning of the Hebrew calendar in 3761 B.C., many bibles from the seventeenth through the twentieth centuries used the date of 4004 B.C., as calculated by Archbishop James Usher. *New Catholic Encyclopedia* (McGraw-Hill, 1997), Vol. 14, p. 498.

Osama bin Laden and his terror network began attacking Americans in the 1990s. He was already wanted for his attacks on two embassies in Africa and the attack on the U.S.S. *Cole* long before 9/11/01. But the adversaries of Christianity begin to multiply greatly at the beginning of the millennary (2000 by modern Western calendars). World War III will be a religious war, with most of the Christian world on one side fighting an enemy alliance formed by non-Christian nations, the Islamic "adversaries of Jesus Christ" which will start to band together and "begin to multiply greatly" near 1996–2000. For a man whose vision spanned the ages, what is near? Certainly we can grant Nostradamus a few years leeway considering that he foresaw this in 1557 and wanted to use a nice even number like "the beginning of the seventh millennary," which is right now.

Quatrain 5:83

Those who will have the enterprise to subvert,

An unparalleled realm, powerful and invincible:

They will act through deceit, three nights to warn,

When the greatest at the table reads his Bible.

The deceitful terrorists try to subvert the mighty America. There are warnings beforehand. The leader of the powerful nation is a Christian.

Osama bin Laden knew America would have to respond, and that American actions will foment hatred and unite the masses of many nations against America. I am thankful that those in power in Washington also understand this probable chain of events, and have not yet given in to Joe Q. Public's cries for immediate and genocidal revenge. The press already reports that the moderate government of Pakistan is in danger of being overthrown by Islamic fundamentalists. They do not support Pakistan's compliance with the United States' attacks on fellow Muslims in Afghanistan. Will terrorists strike again, purposefully leaving evidence that will trace guilt to specific nations; possibly to encourage wider attacks against states that sponsor terrorism like Iraq, Syria, Libya, Sudan, and Iran? It is near the beginning of the millennary, and the enemies of Christianity are about to multiply greatly.

Quatrain 5:70

Of the regions subject to the Balance,
They will trouble the mountains with
 great war,
Captives the entire sex and all Byzantium,
At dawn they will spread the news from
 land to land.

The region of the balance of power, America, will bomb Afghanistan, where there is a war in the mountains and the women are oppressed. The Taliban spread stories of the American attacks throughout the Islamic world to gain support for the anti-American alliance that will eventually rule from Istanbul (Byzantium).

As of mid-October, 2001, the only American (and British) response to the attacks of 9/11/01 has been a limited bombing campaign against Afghanistan. In retaliation, anthrax has been mailed to prominent Americans. It does not require psychic skills to predict that the consequences will be a cycle of retaliation and vengeance that snowballs into a larger war. Many Islamic nations will become even more anti-American, even more united in their determination to bring down "the great Satan" of the United States.

Some years ago my number-one doubt regarding Nostradamus' predicted course of events was the unity of the Islamic world under a leader like Osama bin Laden, who would rule a restored caliphate[18] from Istanbul, Turkey. How would moderate nations such as Turkey be drawn away from NATO alliances and the economic benefits of Western-style democracy by 2002? It didn't make sense that the various nations of the Islamic world, with their different languages, different branches of Islam, different styles of government, and

---

18 Caliphate was the term for the Islamic Empire last ruled by the Ottoman Sultan from Constantinople (now Istanbul) in 1918.

differing political agendas could unify so thoroughly and so quickly.

In the late 1990s the people of Turkey elected an Islamic fundamentalist government to power. The Turkish military staged a coup and prevented them from taking power, but the majority of the Turkish people had voted for the extremists. Many quatrains indicate that the moderate and pro-Western Turkish government will fall prey to the fundamentalists. This is Osama Bin Laden's primary goal in staging the attacks on September 11, 2001—to obtain a harsh American response that will gain sympathy throughout the Islamic world for whoever America bombs, and lead to Islamic unity under the banner of religious fundamentalism and holy war. When this occurs, China will also take advantage of growing anti-American sentiment.

Quatrain 10:72

The year 1999, seventh month,
From the sky will come the great King
   of Terror:
To revive the great king of the Angolmois,
Before and after Mars reigns by good luck.

Basic Interpretation: The great eclipse of 1999 will mark the beginning of Chinese militarism.

Detailed Interpretation: A detailed explanation has already been given linking the total eclipse of the sun in

1999 to the symbolic rebirth of the Mongolian warlord, Genghis Khan, whose tomb was found in China a few months later. As this is the only specific date Nostradamus gives between the French Revolution in 1792 and the end of the world in 3797, he apparently attributes great significance to the changes in Chinese aggression that follow the eclipse of 1999. The incident off the coast of China in 2000 when a Chinese fighter forced an American plane to land at a Chinese base is just the beginning.

Quatrain 3:34

When the eclipse of the sun will then be,
In broad daylight the monster will be seen:
Quite otherwise will it be interpreted,
High price unguarded, none will have
 considered it.

At the time of the eclipse in 1999, the threat, and the future course of events, will be somewhat obvious. But the threat will be misinterpreted, causing unpreparedness when worse events follow. Perhaps the world might assume that China's only territorial goal was the takeover of Hong Kong in 1999. Perhaps the world will think China can be satisfied with the return of Taiwan. Of course the Chinese Army has much greater goals, and will take advantage of the war between Christianity and Islam—but this will not be foreseen or considered until it is too late.

The references above give us the time frame for the start of World War III. France has had fifty-seven years of peace, from 1945 to 2002. An astronomical conjunction in mid-2002 is noted as the time of a big war. Near the beginning of the millennium the enemies of Christianity multiply greatly, and a military power reminiscent of Mongolia's Genghis Khan, probably China, is reawakened after the eclipse of late 1999. Other quatrains describe the first acts of violence and retaliation starting to snowball in late 2001.

Does such an alliance against the West seem reasonable in the near future? Of course it does. China's dictatorship will lose its grip on power if the Internet and the free flow of information so central to the success of American-style capitalism spreads through Chinese society. Fundamentalist Islamic leaders cannot compete economically and at the same time maintain ancient traditions. Non-Americans often hate America because America works, and American progress threatens the traditional way of life they want to maintain.

How can Afghanistan compete in a global economy if their women aren't allowed to read? How can China imitate Hong Kong's economic success without adapting to the information age? How will nations like Iraq make any money to support their people once the oil runs out in a few decades? These nations feel unfairly disenfranchised; their people are just as proud as Americans, and they see a point in history when their way of life is threatened.

They also see the opportunity provided by the general weakness of the once-mighty superpowers. The British Empire once ruled parts of China and the Islamic world. Now the sun has set on the British Empire. The Russian Empire that took over Central Asia's native Muslim peoples and the Soviet Union that took part of Chinese Manchuria at the end of World War II could not defeat Afghanistan between 1979 and 1989. It collapsed in 1991 and has no money, strength, or will power to interfere with Chinese or Islamic aspirations in 2002. And the great Satan itself, the United States of America, was so happy to drastically reduce its military budget after the end of the cold war that two simultaneous conflicts are out of the question. America will not want to fight a world war.

Americans place all their faith in superior technology, ignoring their reduced numbers of soldiers under arms. Chinese technology may lag behind America's, but it can still launch missiles and raise armies. Even if American technological superiority allows battles to end with twice as many Chinese casualties as American ones (or ten times, or a hundred times) how many casualties will the people of the United States be willing to sustain? Communist China could accept war losses of a hundred million troops and still be overpopulated, whereas Americans will protest involvement in a war even before the first coffins come back from the front. No one can match the willingness to fight—and die—of suicidal Islamic terrorists who believe that dying in battle against Americans is a sure ticket to heaven.

This leaves us with a political powder keg waiting to explode. China's vast population can provide tens, even hundreds of millions of troops. The Islamic world adds another billion people to this population base and can supply the oil that armies will need to use in vast quantities, at the same time cutting off the West from those fuel supplies.

Imagine the following scenario: in 2002 repeated acts of terrorism leave trails of evidence pinning blame on Iraq, Syria, and Sudan. America bombs these nations in retaliation. Throughout the Islamic world, millions of Muslims decide events have become an unjust war against Muslims. Islamic fundamentalists overthrow the government of Pakistan as its leaders lose support for aiding too much American aggression against fellow Muslims. Other nations follow suit and more anti-American Islamic fundamentalist governments come to power. (Such seizures of power have barely been prevented already in Algeria, Turkey, and Egypt.) Pakistan definitely has nuclear weapons, and other Islamic nations like Iraq may have nuclear, chemical, or biological weapons as well. America finds itself in a war against a growing number of well-armed Islamic nations and makes plans to increase military spending and reinstitute the draft.

On December 7, 2002, Americans wake up to the news that China has bypassed Taiwan, the expected target of possible Chinese aggression, and has invaded a virtually unarmed Japan overnight. Hundreds of thousands of

Chinese paratroopers with the benefit of surprise have seized most Japanese strategic positions within hours. Chinese forces have been careful to avoid conflict with the few American forces in Japan, even refusing to return fire if fired upon by American soldiers. Chinese leaders claim that China is not at war with the United States; that the new government of Japan has ordered the last pockets of Japanese resistance to surrender; and that any debts (including trillions of dollars from the United States) owed to the old Japanese government are null and void.

Americans wake up with a choice. Which do you think would be the more popular opinion?

A) "Well, the Japanese surprise attacked us that way sixty-one years ago today. I guess it kind of serves them right. I don't think we can handle the war in the Middle East without importing their oil and start a new war against the biggest army in the world and hope to win on their home turf in Asia. The troops at our bases in Japan are as good as dead if we declare war and ignore the Chinese offer to let them leave peacefully. The president is talking about not recognizing the new Chinese-backed government of Japan and placing a trade embargo on China and every place they take over, assuming we can't keep Taiwan or South Korea from going next. I bet the plant will reopen and hire us back if all the competition from Sony and Toyota and Mitsubishi are cut off."

B) "It looks like we'll have to make some big sacrifices
to protect democracy in Asia. You know they'd
do the same for us. After my uncle died fighting
Japan, I'd be proud to have my sons die to protect
them. Besides, companies here thrive on the competition from Asian companies. If we allow Chinese aggression to cut us off from Asian products,
American companies would just grow and grow as
we make our own cars and computer chips and
televisions. And then we could focus on the war in
the Middle East and get that over with. What fun
would that be?"

Neither choice is good, but I think it is very plausible
that the Chinese government knows America has
reduced its military greatly, and cannot handle a world
war like it could have before 1991.

Suddenly the idea of a Third World War in 2002
seems pretty reasonable. In addition to current events
that point in this direction, there are many prophecies
that say the same thing.

Edgar Cayce, the most famous American psychic, foresaw great changes roughly around the year 1998, including the raising up of Xerxes, a reference to a warlord from
the area of Iran and Central Asia, followed by the return
of the messiah.[19] Cayce had also told a boy during
World War II that he would live to see a great religious
war, and that boy is now an old man. The Mayans of

---

19 Lytle Robinson. Edgar Cayce's *Story of the Origin and Destiny of
Man* (Berkley Publishing, New York, 1986), opening page.

Central America had the best calendar in the world, more accurate than that of the modern calendar until the late twentieth century. Their calendar may have been based on an ancient understanding of solar magnetic cycles, their affects on the electromagnetic currents in our brains, and the behavior that solar cycles induce on earth. The Mayans predicted a violent end for our current civilization in December 2012.[20] The Bible has many followers who already expected the end times to begin with the turn of the millennium. In the Book of Revelation two of the main symbols of evil are Babylon (modern-day Iraq) and the "great red dragon"[21]—a fitting symbol for Red (communist) China, with its red flag, red for Communism and the royal color of the Dragon Throne monarchy. China is the only nation that could conceivably raise an army of 200 million troops.[22] The focus of this book, Michel de Nostradamus, obviously describes a war that begins after his native France enjoys fifty-seven years of peace, from 1945 to 2002.

---

20 Adrian Gilbert and Maurice Cotterall. *The Mayan Prophecies* (Barnes & Noble Books, New York, 1995) and John M. Jenkins *Maya Cosmogenesis* 2012 (Bear and Co., Santa Fe, 1998). Author's note: the most basic 11.2-year sunspot cycle does correspond with an 11.2-year cycle in human violence in many regions. Take the area near Iran for example: from 1979–1980 the war in Afghanistan and the war between Iraq and Iran began, then in 1990–1991 the invasions of Kuwait and Iraq, and probably another big war in Afghanistan brewing in 2001, to erupt more massively in 2002—with a cataclysmic change in the level of violence and destruction in late 2012?

21 Revelation 12:3.

22 "The number of troops of cavalry was twice ten thousand times ten thousand," Revelation 9:16.

By now you probably agree that Nostradamus predicts a Third World War for 2002.[23] It is time now to move beyond when it will happen and consider who is involved in the war, where the battles are fought, and what the course and outcome of the war are.

♦   ♦   ♦

---

23 In case you still doubt Nostradamus' prophetic ability, there are more predictions at the end of the book, great examples of his clear successes, but not relevant to World War III.

6

Who Starts the Third World War?

Quatrain 5:54

Of beyond the Black Sea and of the
  great Tartary,
A king comes who will see Gaul,
Piercing across Alania and Armenia,
And within Byzantium he will leave his
  bloody rod.

Basic Interpretation: Osama bin Laden will rule the Islamic alliance from Turkey, and fight into France.

Detailed Interpretation: The Black Sea is halfway between France and Afghanistan, where Osama bin Laden has based his operations. "The great Tartary" further identifies this leader's region as not just slightly beyond the Black Sea, like Armenia, but way beyond it, toward China.

Afghanistan borders China. The leader from this area comes west through the Black Sea coast areas of Armenia and southern Russia (Alania) all the way to France (in Roman times known as Gaul). He will rule from Istanbul, the largest city in Turkey, known as Constantinople when it was a Roman city and Byzantium when it was Greek. This city was once the political center of the Islamic world, and the leader in question would likely be a Muslim. This quatrain indicates that the moderate government of Turkey, currently a democracy and NATO member, will be overthrown by Islamic fundamentalists[24] and shift to the enemy camp that revives an Islamic empire. Quatrains 5:86, 1:40, and 5:25 also indicate the fall of the moderate Turkish government.

The next quatrain, 5:55, seems to be related:

> *In the country of Arabia Felix*
> *One is born powerful in the law of*
>   *Mohammet:*
> *To vex Spain, to conquer Grenada,*
> *And more by sea against the Genoese.*

---

24 Quatrain 5:86 also mentions "Byzantium strongly pressured by the leader of Persia," which could be another reference to Turkey succumbing to Iranian-style Islamic fundamentalism. Quatrain 1:40 says, "The false trumpet concealing madness will bear Byzantium a change of laws." It is another possible reference to the warped fundamentalist version of Islam forcing Turkey to change its government and join the call for holy war. And quatrain 5:25 says, "Byzantium, Egypt, the true serpent invades." Iranian-style Islamic fundamentalist governments will come to power in Turkey and Egypt.

Basic Interpretation: From southern Arabia will come an Islamic leader who will invade Spain.

Detailed Interpretation: The bin Laden family came from the southern Arabian nation of Yemen and moved to southern Saudi Arabia—"Arabia Felix." His family was so rich and influential—so powerful that they were considered a near substitute for the royal family of Saud. In 1979 the Soviets invaded Afghanistan, and America wanted to recruit volunteers from throughout the Islamic world to help their fellow Muslims in Afghanistan fight the Soviet Union. The CIA (and Pakistan's ISI) thought that royal volunteers would help promote the cause, and asked the family of Saud to send a son to Afghanistan. They did not send one of their own, but volunteered Osama bin Laden instead. The situation in Saudi Arabia could be compared to getting a Rockefeller instead of a Kennedy in 1960s America. It still made an impact on the poorer classes of volunteer soldiers, and young Osama was accepted and trained by the ISI and CIA to fight Russians.[25] Don't expect the CIA to acknowledge that they trained him and that their former student uses their training to attack America. Likewise, Osama bin Laden will not be crediting American training for his accomplishments.

Osama bin Laden was born into power, and trained to value the universal brotherhood of Islam—"the law of Mohammet"—more than national ties to Saudi Arabia,

---

25 Joyce M. Davis, et al. Editorials, p. D4, *The Philadelphia Inquirer*, 9/23/2001. Also Kenneth L. Woodward, "A Peaceful Faith, A Fanatic Few" (*Newsweek*, 9/24/01, p. 45).

which has since exiled him. He has become powerful as an Islamic fundamentalist leader, and although born in one nation, now leads men from another nation that happens to be beyond the Black Sea and great Tartary. CNN has shown his supporters celebrating America's humiliation across the Islamic world, from Pakistanis to Palestinians. Coincidence? Few people ever come to power outside the nation in which they are born, but the leader Nostradamus describes does. He will conquer Grenada, an Islamic kingdom in Spain until 1492, and intimidate the entire Spanish nation. Italy will also be invaded.

Quatrain 3:20

Through the opposite sides of the great river
  Betique
Far in Iberia to the Kingdom of Grenada
Crosses repulsed by the Mohammetans
One of Cordova will betray his country.

Basic Interpretation: Muslim armies are victorious over Christian forces at locations in Spain.

Detailed Interpretation: Betique is the Latin name for the Guadalquivir River in Spain. Grenada and Cordoba are also in Spain. Spain and Portugal make up the Iberian peninsula. The Moslem followers of Mohammed push back Christian defenders of the cross, and are helped by a traitor in Cordoba. In quatrain 8:51 Nostradamus clarifies that the leader who takes Cordoba is Byzantine—ruling from Istanbul. The invaders are not just from nearby

North Africa, but from a vast alliance ruled from Turkey. This leader decides that an Islamic invasion of southern Spain could prevent the American and British navies from entering the Mediterranean if the Straits of Gibraltar are effectively sealed off. The idea that Muslims would attack Spain before dealing with Israel right in the core of their Middle Eastern center of power seems odd at first, but perhaps sealing the Straits first prevents the Western navies from coming to Israel's aid.

Paragraph 34 of the letter to King Henry II:

> *And a new incursion will be made by the maritime shores, determined to deliver the Sierra Morena from the first Mohammetan recapture. Their assaults will not all be in vain, and the place which was once the abode of Abraham will be assaulted by those who hold Jupiter in veneration.*

Basic Interpretation: Muslim forces will capture Spain, Westerners retake it, but Israel then falls.

Detailed Interpretation: The Sierra Morena is a mountain range in southern Spain. Muslims recapture it (for the first time) after 510 years under Christian control. Western naval invasions come to retake Spain, but the Muslims' assault into Spain is not in vain, for the distraction allows the pagan followers of Jupiter (as Nostradamus sometimes refers to Muslims) to conquer Israel, the land of Abraham. Freed from the Israeli distraction in their midst, the forces of Islam can then attack Europe in force.

Quatrain 8:96

The sterile synagogue without any fruit
Will be received by the infidels:
The daughter of the persecuted of Babylon,
Miserable and sad her wings will be clipped.

Basic Interpretation: Israel will be conquered by her Islamic neighbors after they defeat her air force.

Detailed Interpretation: Synagogues will be empty of people; they will be taken over by infidels—Muslims. Ancient Israel was captured by Babylon and the Jews were exiled there. Modern Israel, "The daughter of the persecuted of Babylon," is again defeated and powerless, her people oppressed, and possibly exterminated.[26] This may seem unrealistic to people who have watched the well-trained Israelis repeatedly defeat the larger forces of their Islamic neighbors. But in the last war (1973) the Arabs initially did very well, and the Israeli Air Force (the wings that are clipped), so critical to the nation's defense, had a third of its planes shot down. The Arabs threw caution to the wind and allowed ground forces to advance beyond the protective cover of their anti-aircraft missiles, after which they were massacred. Cautious and more complete use of surface-to-air missiles in the next war could lead Israel's larger neighbors to victory

---

26 Remember the first example of the clearest Nostradamian success: the collapse of the Soviet Union in seventy-three years and seven months? Those sentences mention that the Soviet Union was enlarged by the *first* holocaust.

over it—especially if Palestine gains some independence and the Islamic forces can build up and begin the war deep in what had been Israeli territory in 1973. The next war there will see Israel defeated before the West eventually liberates it, probably because Israel can no longer rely on a superior air force against overwhelming numbers of ground troops. Jet fighters are no match for faster antiaircraft missiles, and stealth technology is nearly worthless.[27]

Nostradamus tells us that the war will be started by followers of Mohammet; by Arabians and Iranians and Turks and Algerians and Tunisians. They will be led by Osama bin Laden, born in southern Arabia and operating from Afghanistan before moving on to Turkey. The initial course of battle involves the first Islamic reconquest of Spain, more to seal off the entrance to the Mediterranean that to establish a permanent front. Western forces land to take Spain back, but meanwhile Israel falls. This will allow the Muslim armies to make a more focused push into southern Europe, especially Spain and Italy.

♦ ♦ ♦

27 If you've seen *Star Trek* movies you probably remember watching Klingon ships cloak themselves to hide—but you can still see where they are because the silhouette of their ships are completely black, devoid of stars—unlike the space around them. Likewise, while radar is ineffective for seeing stealth aircraft, Chinese technicians realized that by looking for holes in a sky full of background radio noise, they could tell exactly where American stealth aircraft were flying.

7

Crusade and Jihad

Such a war will pit the Christian world on one side and the Islamic world on the other. Nostradamus, a devout Catholic, viewed the enemies of Christianity as infidels, barbarians, and antichrists. Many authorities on this subject portray the three antichrists mentioned by Nostradamus as Napoleon, Hitler, and some as-yet undesignated Muslim leader in World War III. But this is incorrect. Nostradamus clearly describes all three antichrists in the scope of World War III. Various Islamic leaders fill this role over the course of a long conflict.

Quatrain 10:66

The chief of London through the realm of
*   America,*
The Isle of Scotland tempered by frost:

> *King and Reb will face such a treacherous*
> *antichrist,*
> *That he will place everyone in the conflict.*

Basic Interpretation: Britain and America will fight an antichrist whose treachery starts a large war.

Detailed Interpretation: Britain and America were also allies in the first two world wars, but America was brought into these wars through Britain's need for help against Germany. This time Britain is involved through an attack on America. The rebellious Americans that fought for independence from Britain's king in the eighteenth century became close allies in the twentieth century. They will be allied with the British in a war against an antichrist who brings the world to war through treachery. This describes World War II to a certain degree, but Nostradamus did not describe Hitler as an antichrist, and Hitler did not attack Britain or America. The British declared war on Germany, and Japan's attack on Pearl Harbor brought America into World War II. Scottish frost aside (perhaps an especially cold winter to come in 2002?) this quatrain seems like a clear description of Tony Blair's support for America after Osama bin Laden's terrorist attacks on New York and Washington. America and Britain were the first nations to bomb terrorist bases in Afghanistan, but a larger coalition of nations—"everyone"—will fight them later.

Paragraph 23–24 of the letter to King Henry II:

> *Then the great Empire of the Antichrist*
> *will begin where once was Atilla's empire and*
> *Xerxes will descend with great and countless*
> *numbers, that the coming of the Holy Ghost,*
> *proceeding from the 48th degree, will make a*
> *transmigration, chasing out the abomination*
> *of the Antichrist, who will have made war*
> *against the great Vicar and the Church of*
> *Jesus Christ, and whose reign will be for a*
> *time and to the end of time. This will be*
> *preceded by a solar eclipse . . .*

Basic Interpretation: The leader from the region of Afghanistan, (with the spirit of the antichrist) raises a huge army that attacks Christianity. This leads a Christian ruler (with the spirit of the Holy Ghost) from the region of 48 degrees north latitude, to chase this antichrist out of Europe. This will happen not too long after the eclipse of August 1999.

Detailed Interpretation: Osama bin Laden, the first of three human hosts of the spirit of the antichrist, will raise an army starting in central Asia and Iran where Atilla and Xerxes came from. The huge army he raises will make war against Christian Europe, which will be defended by someone from 48 degrees north, embodying the spirit of the Holy Ghost. Geneva is near 48 degrees north—

perhaps the United Nations will have a great leader—but Paris, Munich, Budapest, and many other cities are also near this latitude. The Christian leader could be from any location, and just speak at the United Nations before acting, or act through the auspices of the U.N. Shortly before these events (remember Nostradamus wrote this letter in 1557—to him, the eclipse of August 1999 is shortly before 2001–2002), there will be a solar eclipse. The antichrist will "reign for a time and to the end of time." This demonstrates that while one man may embody the evil of the antichrist for a few short years, evil itself, and the idea of antichrists, lasts forever. Osama bin Laden is merely the first antichrist of World War III.

Quatrain 9:44

Leave, leave Geneva every one,
Saturn will be changed from gold to iron,
Those against RAYPOZ will all be
*   exterminated,*
Before the coming the Heavens will show
*   signs.*

Basic Interpretation: A traitor will destroy the United Nations in Geneva.

Detailed Interpretation: People will want to leave Geneva, and probably the United Nations, child of Geneva's League of Nations. This will happen when the golden age of peace (1945–2002) changes to a time of war—iron. Saturn is the Roman name for the Greek Chronos, father time. In these changing times a traitor will kill his enemies. RAY-POZ is an anagram for Zopyra, who tricked the Babylonians and allowed that city's capture by his king, Darius of Persia. Perhaps someone will trick Geneva (the United Nations) into believing one thing when, in fact, great danger and imminent invasion from the Middle East are coming. Perhaps many Islamic nations will leave the United Nations in protest of some American retaliation against Islamic terrorism, and the remaining delegations in Geneva will only be from nations that support America. Then a traitorous U.N. delegation truly loyal to Osama bin Laden, but pretending not to be, might blow up the U.N. and exterminate only his enemies, possibly including hostages like Ambassador Negroponte. The traitor may be a woman in a foreign delegation, as Nostradamus wrote in quatrain 5:12 that "near Lake Geneva it will be conducted, by the young girl foreign wishing to betray the city." Before this betrayal, events in the sky (like the planes that crashed into the World Trade Center's twin towers) will foretell the fate of Geneva at terrorists' hands. This may be the incident at 48 degrees north that brings the spirit of the Holy Ghost into play.

Quatrain 9:60

Conflict Barbarian in the black Headdress,
Blood shed, Dalmatia to tremble:
Great Ishmael will set up his promontory,
Frogs to tremble, aid Lusitanian.

Basic Interpretation: War in Yugoslavia starts again.

Detailed Interpretation: Muslims often wear headdresses and were considered barbarians by the Christians of Nostradamus' time. Osama bin Laden has worn white and black turbans. Dalmatia was a Roman province in modern Yugoslavia, roughly corresponding to Bosnia. Perhaps the Serbs attempt more ethnic cleansing in the region, expecting no interference in the beginning of a holy war when the West is unlikely to defend Muslims. Ishmael was a son of the biblical Abraham from whom the Arab peoples claim descent, so "Great Ishmael" probably means all his Arab descendants, i.e., the Middle East. Arabs establish a toehold—a promontory—in Europe, but not necessarily in Yugoslavia—probably in southern Spain. "Frog" is a derogatory reference to the French; perhaps they realize the building threat from the millions of Arab immigrants already in France and the invasion of Spain means trouble for them as well. Lusitania was the Roman name for Portugal, so apparently Portugal offers what little help it can to Spain. But it is also possible that the Portuguese-speaking nation of Brazil, Portugal's greatest legacy from colonial times, is the one that sends aid. Brazil was the only South American nation that contributed troops to the Allied cause throughout World War II, and perhaps in World War III that devoutly Catholic nation will realize that an Islamic threat to Europe is a threat to all the Christian nations.

Quatrain 8:48

Saturn in Cancer, Jupiter with Mars,
In February Chaldondon Salvaterre,
Sault, Castalon assailed from three sides,
Near Verbiesque conflict mortal war.

Basic Interpretation: The only clear reference is an invasion of Spain.

Detailed Interpretation: "Jupiter with Mars" probably means that Jupiter, the pagan (Muslim) leader, is at war (with Mars). *Chaldondon* probably means Chaldean, which could mean a soothsayer (storyteller)—for which the region of ancient Chaldea was famous—or it could just mean someone from that region, once known as Babylonia and now Iraq. *Salvaterre* translates as "safe land." Perhaps after a decade of allied bombs falling on Iraq, World War III actually takes the pressure off Iraq and it is a safe land again. *Sault* is an old French word for rapids, *Castalon* describes the region as Castile in central Spain. It may be a reference to the Sierra Morena mountain range in southern Spain.[28] *Verbiesque*, according to some other authors,[29] could mean Serbia. There will be a war going on near Serbia when the Muslims are first landing in Spain.

---

28 *Saltus Castulonensis* is the Roman name for the Sierra Morenas (Leoni, ibid., pp. 362–363).

29 The original source of this possible decoding may be Rolfe Boswell, whose *Nostradamus Speaks* (see p. 156) came out in 1941.

Paragraph 44 of the letter to King Henry II:

> *In the Adriatic will arise great discord, and*
> *that which was united will be separated. To a*
> *house will be reduced that which was, and is,*
> *a great city, including the Pampotamia and*
> *Mesopotamia of Europe at 45, and others of*
> *41, 42, and 37 degrees.*

Basic Interpretation: War in Yugoslavia flares up again, and four cities are destroyed with nuclear weapons.

Detailed Interpretation: Nostradamus is from southern France, and because of this, most details of the upcoming war describe France, Spain, and Italy. But by the 1990s a war has already been under way between Christians and Muslims for many years—in Yugoslavia. Yugoslavia, which was united but is now separated. Yugoslavia, with its only coastline on the Adriatic Sea. The Western press never wrote much about foreign involvement there, but tens of thousands of Turks, Pakistanis, Iranians, and other Muslim troops helped Muslim Albanians and Bosnians fight the Serbs. Muslims hate the Serbs for the ethnic cleansing that occurred in Yugoslavia. If the Serbs think they can continue ethnic cleansing without being bombed again by Americans—because America will be busy fighting Muslims as well, then the Serbians might start another war against Muslim Albanians, Kosovars, or Bosnians. They might do it just because they see the lines being drawn between Muslims and Christians and see no point in delaying the inevitable and allowing the Muslims in the Balkans time to improve their defenses, but Serbian actions may lead to nuclear retaliation from Muslim nations that have watched Serbia with growing hatred for over a decade already.

The Serbian capital of Belgrade is at 45 degrees north latitude. Serbia has been the most warlike nation in Europe in recent years; the Serb government in Belgrade may merit the title of Pampotamia for their aggression. Belgrade does sit between the Sava and Danube Rivers, making it a Mesopotamia, literally "land between two rivers." Logically, a dying Israel might be the first to use nuclear weapons, but Israel's targets would be cities like Damascus, (33 degrees) Cairo, (30 degrees) or Baghdad (33 degrees). The targets Nostradamus mentions are too far north, and the one at 45 degrees is in Europe.

Assuming that four cities reduced to houses will be attacked with nuclear warheads near these latitudes, they will probably all be in the Mediterranean area near the start of a Muslim invasion of southern Europe. There might be a two-stage, tit-for-tat retaliation in which two Muslim and two Christian cities are attacked. If I am forced to guess which cities will suffer such nuclear assaults, I will assume that Muslims (who have Turkey on their side by this time) would nuke Belgrade at 45, then NATO would bomb Algiers at 37, the Muslims would bomb Rome at 42, and then NATO would destroy Istanbul at 41. I hope that such madness does not come to pass, but even if it does, other cities could be meant instead.

Quatrain 8:99

Through the power of the three temporal
  Kings,
In another place the sacred see will be put:
Where the substance of the corporal spirit
Will be delivered and received as the true seat.

Three political leaders (probably the three antichrists of World War III) will cause the Holy See of the Papacy to be relocated. I expect "another place" for the pope to relocate will be in Brazil, a Catholic nation whose people will proudly restore and receive the true seat if Rome is destroyed and Europe is not safe.

Quatrain 2:41

For seven days the great star will burn,
The cloud shall make two suns to appear:
The big mastiff will howl all night
When the great pontiff changes country.

Basic Interpretation: Rome is destroyed in a nuclear explosion and the papacy has to relocate.

Detailed Interpretation: A nuclear fireball does look much like the large one we know as the sun, and this image of two suns is caused by a (mushroom?) cloud. A great star burns, maybe the shining example of once-glorious Rome? Someone howls in outrage. Nostradamus once used the term "mastiff," often interpreted to refer to Winston Churchill, the British Bulldog—but as in many quatrains, the possibilities here are too numerous to determine now, even if the explanation will seem obvious with the benefit of future hindsight. The pope is forced to relocate to a new country. Rome, the symbolic seat of Christianity, is almost certainly targeted for nuclear destruction, a likely event when Islamic nations start a holy war against the West. Rome is also at 42 degrees, one of four latitudes Nostradamus mentioned in the Letter to King Henry II where cities have special destruction to come.

There are several major points to make regarding the nuclear elimination of four cities:

♦ After the world realizes that a nuclear tit-for-tat loss of cities could go on forever with no positive benefits to either side, the war will probably remain conventional, and be fought more with gunpowder than uranium. This takes away the nuclear advantage the West has.

♦ Nostradamus is very clear that the papacy will be relocated away from Rome (one of his three themes throughout his prophecies), suggesting the move be to the safety of the Americas, for in quatrain 4:50 he writes that "Libra will see the Hesperias reign, having the monarchy of heaven and earth." "The Hesperias" is an ancient poetic term for the lands of the West, and the only "monarchy of heaven and earth" that any American nation would accept would be the papacy, probably in one of the large Catholic nations of Latin America like Brazil.[30]

◆ If Istanbul is bombed, and Osama bin Laden was ruling from Istanbul, the new capital of the revived caliphate, it would make sense that he finally dies. Thus ends the rule of the first antichrist.

Paragraph 45 of the letter to King Henry II:

> *At this time and in these countries that the infernal power will set against the Church of Jesus Christ the power of its adversaries. This will be the second Antichrist, who will persecute that Church and its true Vicar, by means of the power of three temporal kings who through ignorance are seduced by tongues, which will cut more than any sword in the hands of madmen.*

Basic Interpretation: After Rome and Istanbul are attacked, a *second* antichrist comes to power.

Detailed Interpretation: There may be a propaganda war of treacherous tongues in which Muslims encourage

---

30 Not only would Brazil be a logical choice, as it is the most populous Catholic nation and far from the front lines of World War III, but this would coincide with other prophecies like those of the twelfth-century Irish monk, St. Malachy, who wrote a list of all future popes of Rome. Various sources on St. Malachy claim Pope John Paul II is the third or second to last pope, that the last (next?) one is black, and that Rome is destroyed when he is pope. If the Vatican relocates to Brazil, it seems possible that a darker-skinned man will become pope, and renounce destroyed Rome as the seat of the Church.

Christians not to accept a new Brazilian pope. This new pope may be hastily elected under questionable circumstances when Rome, the College of Cardinals, and normal Church procedures are understandably bypassed. I'm reminded of the day Ronald Reagan was shot, and Alexander Haig yelled out, "I'm in charge." I don't blame him for attempting to end the chaos and offer a sense of stability to a nation in doubt, but he was not in charge. Likewise the Catholic world may need someone to offer immediate leadership, even if that leadership is disputed later. It probably will be disputed, because racism is an issue, and many will not accept a dark-skinned pope. The three temporal kings could be European leaders, causing a rift in the Church, or more likely just the three antichrists Nostradamus mentions. In any event, paragraph 45 points out that the pen will be mightier than the sword in causing trouble for the leader of the Catholic Church at this time.

◆　◆　◆

8

A Very Modern War

Many quatrains describe the weapons and mass destruction of World War III in convincingly modern detail, like the (mushroom) cloud and second sun appearing when Rome is destroyed. Nostradamus describes aerial combat, catastrophic losses, and nuclear devastation in great detail, which also removes any doubt that such prophecies were meant for earlier periods in time.

Quatrain 1:64

At night they will think they have seen
the sun
When the pig half-man they will see:
Noise, chanting, battle, fighting in the sky,
And the brute beasts talking will be heard.

A nuclear fireball again creates the illusion of another sun at night. The "pig half-man" could be a nickname for a vile political leader. Fighting in the sky is the crucial arena of modern battle. Hearing brute beasts talking may merely mean we hear weapons being used.

Quatrain 1:72

Of Marseilles the inhabitants completely changed,
Flight and pursuit up to near Lyons,
Narbonne, Toulouse through Bordeaux outraged:
Killed and captives almost a million.

Southeastern France is occupied, with a retreat of French forces northward, pursued from Marseilles toward Lyon. The new inhabitants are probably North African immigrants and foreign troops. Perhaps supplies from the Atlantic port city of Bordeaux are held back for local defenses when badly needed in Narbonne and Toulouse. Losses of a million people have never occurred in southern France before, so the events must be part of a horrible future war.

Quatrain 2:91

At sunrise a great fire shall be seen,
Noise and light towards Aquilon extending:
Within the circle death and cries one will hear,
Through sword, fire, famine, death awaiting them.

Only huge modern explosions kill within a circle; older weapons like arrows and guns all kill in a linear path. War will spread toward Russia, probably as Islamic fundamentalists take over small nations that were once Soviet Republics, such as Turkmenistan in Central Asia or Azerbaijan in the Caucasus.

Quatrain 2:96

Burning torch in the sky will be seen at night
Near the end and beginning of the Rhone:
Famine, sword: late the relief provided,
The Persian again invades Macedonia.

Burning torches in the skies of Geneva and Marseilles are evidence of aerial warfare in southeastern France, an area hardly touched by the first two world wars. Famine and late relief may be the result of the previously mentioned delay in supplies from Bordeaux. Iran is simultaneously invading Macedonia (southeastern Europe) for the first time in over twenty centuries.

Quatrain 3:11

The arms to fight in the sky a long time,
The tree in the middle of the city fallen:
Vermin itch, steel, in the face of the
*   firebrand,*
Then the monarch of Adria fallen.

At a time of aerial combat, a large structure falls in Paris. "The city" usually means Paris when Nostradamus writes it; perhaps bombings will destroy the Eiffel Tower—"the tree in the middle of the city." War, and defeat for a leader of Venice, or all of Italy or an area near the Adriatic Sea occur.

Quatrain 5:8

There will be unleashed live fire, hidden death,
Within the globes horrible and frightful,
By night the fleet lets go, the city to powder,
The city afire, the enemy favorable.

Atoms are made of tiny globelike particles that can unleash an incredible firestorm. Such nuclear weapons can be (and probably will be, to minimize travel time that gives warning and opportunities to be intercepted) launched from submarines close to their targets and can literally reduce a city to dust. We could not expect a clearer description of a nuclear attack. As atomic bombs were dropped on Japan in the daytime, and not from a ship, such nuclear warfare is yet to come. Nuclear reduction to powder is so bad that occupation by the enemy would be preferable to the survivors.

◆　◆　◆

9

How Does the War Proceed?

So far the war seems very bleak. Osama bin Laden, Nostradamus' first antichrist, starts a jihad against the West and unites the Islamic world. Islamic forces eventually ally with China. Superior Western technology does not prevent nuclear destruction of Rome and other cities, and a conventional invasion destroys Israel and devastates southern Europe. How does the war develop after the initial bad start? It gets worse before it gets better, because after a limited nuclear exchange that destroys cities like Rome and Istanbul, Saddam Hussein may be the second antichrist to lead the Islamic alliance after Osama bin Laden's death.

Quatrain 8:70

The villain will enter wicked, infamous,
Tyrannizing over Mesopotamia:
All friends made by the dame of adulterous
*   parentage,*
Land horrible black of physical features.

Basic Interpretation: Saddam Hussein rules Iraq despite the U.N. coalition and the Gulf War.

Detailed Interpretation: Mesopotamia is the ancient name for Iraq. The current infamous tyrant, Saddam Hussein, fits the first two lines nicely. "All friends" probably refers to the alliance of nations that fought Iraq in 1991. The United Nations is the dame and its predecessor, the League of Nations that Nostradamus has so little respect for, is the bastard parentage. The land was blackened by the destruction of war, and especially by burning oil. Hussein may enter Europe under conditions similar to those of Kuwait in 1991, and this time some of the friends of the United Nations will see Europe blackened.

Quatrain 2:30

One who the infernal gods of Hannibal
Will cause to be reborn, terror of mankind
Never more horror or worse news
Than will come through Babel to the
  Romans.

Basic Interpretation: Saddam Hussein will be the second antichrist and will destroy Italy.

Detailed Interpretation: Hannibal was from Carthage (North Africa) and conquered parts of Italy. Babel (Babylon) was in Iraq. Both are key regions in the Muslim world, and apparently a barbaric leader from these areas will come to invade Italy as Hannibal once did. As

Nostradamus says that the infernal gods of pagans cause the rebirth of this terror of mankind, it seems this Iraqi leader is the second antichrist of World War III.

Quatrain 7:6

Naples, Palermo, and all Sicily,
Through hand Barbarian it will be
depopulated:
Corsica, Salerno, and the Isle of Sardinia,
Famine, plague, war, end of evils extended.

Basic Interpretation: Muslims will devastate southern Italy.

Detailed Interpretation: Muslims (barbarians) will either kill the inhabitants of the west coast of Italy or scare them into evacuating. The depopulation could result from the use of underwater nuclear detonations that would flood the region of western Italy and the islands of Sicily, Sardinia, and Corsica. Famine, plague, and war are self-evident.

Quatrain 1:9

From the Orient will come the Punic heart
To anger Adria and the heirs of Romulus,
Accompanied by the Libyan fleet,
Malta to tremble and the neighboring isles
empty.

Basic Interpretation: Middle Eastern armies enter Italy.

Detailed Interpretation: Rome fought the Punic Wars against Carthage, near modern-day Tunis. Punic probably refers to anything from North Africa. "From the Orient"—the East—implies a people from no closer than the Middle East. This will come to Italy, represented by the Italian cities that once ruled empires: Venice, once known as Adria, and Rome, as Romulus and Remus are the mythical founders of Rome. So armies from the Middle East, with a heart or a leader likened to the North African leader Hannibal, Rome's archenemy during the Punic Wars, will attack Italy and nearby isles. Quatrain 2:30 already suggests that Saddam Hussein is Hannibal reborn, apparently Iraq and other Middle Eastern forces are accompanied by naval help from Libyans and other North Africans. Malta trembles but the bigger islands to the north are already depopulated.

Quatrain 2:86

Shipwrecked fleet near the Adriatic Sea:
The land trembles moved into the air placed
on land:
Egypt trembles Mohammetan increase,
The Herald is sent to ask for surrender.

Basic Interpretation: A shipwreck precedes political turmoil in Egypt and a call for surrender.

Detailed Interpretation: Near the Adriatic Sea must mean south of it, as land surrounds its other sides. So between southern Italy and western Greece (possibly near Malta) a fleet is shipwrecked. Islamic fundamentalism grows even stronger in Egypt, perhaps a moderate Egyptian leader is blamed for the naval losses. Someone may request a formal surrender, or this may be another reference to Islam, which in Arabic means surrender or submission. Perhaps both meanings are correct, and a somewhat moderate Egyptian government is replaced by Islamic fundamentalists.

Quatrain 5:14

Saturn and Mars in Leo Spain captive,
By the Libyan chief trapped in the conflict,
Near Malta, Herode captured alive,
The Roman sceptre will be astonished by
   the Cock.

Basic Interpretation: The war in Spain bogs down a North African army, and an enemy of Christ is captured at sea. Italy is surprised by the actions of the French leader.

Detailed Interpretation: At the time of a very common astronomical conjunction Spain will be invaded by someone from North Africa who will be delayed on the Spanish front. Another Muslim leader, an enemy of Christianity as King Herod was, will be captured at sea near the small island of Malta—alive. Or perhaps the Libyan chief responsible for the Muslim armies in Spain is also the man caught at sea. Here, in quatrain 5:14, the Libyan is a chief, but there is a Libyan fleet in quatrain 1:9 in the same time frame. In quatrain 8:51 there is a Byzantine (Turkish) leader captured at sea after Cordoba has been seized. While the homeland of the Islamic naval commander is uncertain, such a man is captured at sea after the Muslim reconquest of southern Spain.

"The Roman sceptre"—Italian power—is snubbed by France, as the cock was a symbol that represented the ancient Gauls. Perhaps the French will consider themselves the leaders of Europe and demand that the captured Libyan Herode be sent to France. More in tune with defense supplies being withheld at Bordeaux, perhaps there will be various defense plans for Europe, including one plan to defend central Italy, but the French will veto that plan and make their defensive line further north, abandoning central Italy to the enemy.

Quatrain 2:93

Very near the Tiber presses the Goddess of Death:
Shortly before the great inundation:
The chief of the ship taken, thrown into the well:
Castle, palace in conflagration.

Basic Interpretation: Near Rome there is great violence before a huge flood. Fire and chaos on land.

Detailed Interpretation: The Tiber River in central Italy will be near the front line of battle just before a great flood. Someone is thrown into the well, sink, or sewer-pipe, depending on the translation. Probably the captured Herode is a North African naval commander who is drowned by the Italians, as he has caused others to drown. If "the chief of the ship" means the pope, as the leader of that Christian ship, the Bark of St. Peter, it seems unlikely the pope would be forcibly drowned. War, fire, and flood to come.

Quatrain 2:81

*Through fire from the sky the city almost
   burned:
The urn threatens another Decaulion:
Sardinia will be vexed by the Punic foist,
After Libra abandons her Phaethon.*

Basic Interpretation: Another flood is near, and Italian islands are attacked by North Africans.

Detailed Interpretation: Paris ("the city") is almost or partially destroyed. Perhaps a missile lands in the suburbs or is blown up in the atmosphere before hitting its target. The urn refers to a large container, and since Decaulion is the biblical flood, it seems that the sea will rise from its Mediterranean bowl and flood the land at the time of a North African (Punic) invasion of Sardinia. Libra is the balance. Phaethon, in Greek myth, is the son of Apollo and borrowed his father's sun chariot but could not control it. So if it appears that the balance of the sun's path through the sky is lost, perhaps people are seeing the false suns of nuclear explosions. Perhaps the following tactic will be used in World War III: set off a nuclear detonation several miles out to sea, off the coast of a target city. The tidal wave would wipe out the enemy city just the same as bombing it directly, without the intense radioactivity that would make the site uninhabitable. This would preserve the usefulness of the area and allow colonization after victory. Woe to Italy if this is done to the Italian coast.

Quatrain 10:60

I weep for Nice, Monaco, Pisa, Genoa,
Savona, Siena, Capua, Modena, Malta:
The above blood and sword for a new year's
   gift
Fire, the earth to tremble, water, unfortunate
   unwillingness.

Basic Interpretation: Near the turn of the new year (2003?) the west coast of Italy is destroyed.

Detailed Interpretation: The coastline from southeastern France to southernmost Italy is destroyed by a combination of warfare, fire, earthquakes, and flood, possibly through the use of nuclear weapons detonated at sea[31] to cause tidal waves on coastlines. There is an "unfortunate unwillingness" to evacuate before the new year.

Quatrain 2:4

From Monaco to near Sicily,
All of the seaside will remain desolated:
There will remain no suburb, city, or village
That by Barbarians is not pillaged and
    robbed.

Interpretation: The entire west coast of Italy will suffer under the Islamic invader's onslaught.

Quatrain 1:18

Through the Gallic discord and negligence
A passage to Mohammed will be opened:
Steeped in blood the land of Siena,
The Phocaean port covered with ships
    and sails.

Basic Interpretation: French incompetence allows the Muslim invasion, and Marseilles' port is kept busy.

Detailed Interpretation: The Gallic people of France will apparently argue over the seriousness of the Islamic

---

31 This could be what Nostradamus means in quatrain 9:100 when he writes: "Fire in the ships to the West ruin: New trick. . . ."

threat and neglect to defend their nation through adequate immigration restrictions or military preparedness, as previously noted for quatrain 1:73. Siena is northwest of Rome, and perhaps France's unwillingness to defend central Italy (as noted for quatrain 5:14) opens a passage to Mohammed there as well. The French port of Marseilles was founded by Greek Phocaeans, and will be extremely busy when Muslim armies are at war with the nations of southern Europe.

Quatrain 3:90

The great Satyr and Tiger of Hyrcanie,
Gift presented to those of the Ocean:
A chief of the fleet leaves from Carmania,
Who will take land at the Tyrren Phocaean.

Basic Interpretation: An Iranian admiral lands in southern France.

Detailed Interpretation: A satyr is a mythical man-beast. Nostradamus considers this Iranian admiral from the area east of Teheran (the ancient Persian province of Hyrcania) to be a viscous animal. Fortune apparently favors this fleet as it leaves the old province of Carmania, on the southeast coast of modern Iran. This Iranian fleet lands at Marseilles, implying the full cooperation of modern-day Egypt—for without use of the Suez canal

---

32 Quatrain 8:34 mentions "floods and dusky ones seven million" during battles near the Swiss border.

this fleet would have an extremely long trip around Africa.

Quatrain 1:73

France on five sides through neglect assailed,
Tunis, Algiers deeply moved by Persians:
Leon, Seville, Barcelona already failed,
There is no fleet from the Venetians.

Basic Interpretation: North African armies plow through Spain and into France.

Detailed Interpretation: France is attacked from various directions, quite possibly a result of sabotage by the millions of Algerians, Moroccans, and Tunisians currently living in France and comprising anywhere from 10–20 percent of France's population, depending on figures for illegal immigrants. This may be where Nostradamus gets the figure of seven million for the number of dark-skinned foreigners fighting near the Juras mountains.[32]

Probably because of lax military preparedness and lax immigration laws and enforcement, France will be overrun by hostile Islamic forces. Persia (Iran) is where Islamic fundamentalism first took hold in 1979, and Iran has worked hard to spread religious fundamentalism and anti-Westernism to other Islamic nations, especially Sudan, Algeria, Turkey, and Egypt. Apparently Iranian extremism will take hold in Tunisian and Algerian populations, both in their own militaries in North

Africa—and probably among saboteurs in France as well, although Nostradamus does not specify a traitor as he did for Spain. Perhaps he does not consider the Muslim immigrants to France as true Frenchmen, merely as a first wave of the invasion, hence they are not traitors to France. The major cities of Spain will already have been conquered by the Muslim invaders by the time France is invaded. Venice, which had a powerful navy in Nostradamus' time and defended Europe from the Turkish fleet, will have no empire or fleet in 2002, and offers no protection as they did in centuries past.

Quatrain 2:29

The Easterner will leave his seat,
To pass the Appenine mountains to see Gaul:
Transpiercing the sky, the waters and snow,
And everyone will be struck with his stick.

Basic Interpretation: The brutal Islamic leader will come to see France.

Detailed Interpretation: The Eastern leader will leave his capital and cross the mountains of southern Italy before advancing into France. This will happen during winter (snow) and involve aerial combat in the sky. His violence will affect everyone.

Quatrain 9:73

Into Foix enters the Blue-Turbaned King,
And he will reign less than a revolution
of Saturn:
White-Turbaned King to Byzantium heart
exiled,
Sun, Mars, Mercury near Aquarius.

Basic Interpretation: The Muslim alliance changes its commander in chief.

Detailed Interpretation: Foix is a town in southwest France. The Muslim commander who enters it is probably North African, as Berbers sometimes wear blue turbans but most Muslims wear white or black ones.[33] This Islamic leader will rule before the war has lasted an orbit of Saturn—before twenty-nine years have gone by.

I do not interpret this to mean the war will last almost twenty-nine years after 2002, however. Nostradamus repeatedly uses multiple dating systems that contradict each other, and in this case are best reconciled if he does not mean that World War III lasts twenty-nine years, but only means that the Holy War between Islam and Christianity lasts almost twenty-nine years. There are many dates that could be designated for the beginning of this period, but Osama bin Laden's choice is 1979, when he

---

33 This is supported by quatrain 6:80, which describes those of the cross pursuing to death "blues" that have invaded Europe from Fez, a region in Morocco.

first went to Afghanistan to defend it from the Russians. The *mujahadeen* (Arabic for "those who wage Holy War") obviously chose their name based on the view that their defense of Afghanistan was the start of a Holy War. If so, the blue-turbaned Islamic leader may come to power around 2004, after about twenty-five years of Holy War.

The former commander with a white turban is punished by being sent to Byzantium—now Istanbul.[34] If Istanbul were still a great city and the capital of a revived caliphate this would not be punishment, it would be a promotion. The fact that it is punishment confirms the earlier destruction of Istanbul. Whether this leader is sent to rebuild the city or rebuild the idea of the caliphate is hard to say. The conjunction in the fourth line remains unsolved.

Quatrain 3:93

In Avignon the chief of all the empire
Will stop on the way to desolated Paris:
Tricast will hold the anger of Hannibal:
Lyons will be poorly consoled for the change.

Basic Interpretation: The Muslim leader will stop in southern France.

---

34 Quatrain 2:2 reads: "The blue head will inflict upon the white head as much of evil as France did them good," indicating two points. First, the North Africans—to whom French rule brought modern civilization—will mistreat France under North African rule. Second, the blue-turbaned leader will punish the white-turbaned leader.

Detailed Interpretation: Avignon is a symbolic religious site in southeastern France that was once home to popes. The chief of the Muslim empire probably stops there as a symbol of the conquest of Christianity. Paris is destroyed and/or evacuated. Quatrain 2:81 already mentioned that Paris was almost burned through fire from the sky. Tricast may be the town of Troyes (Tricasses, in Roman times) and the defenders there probably offer stiff resistance that slows down the Islamic advance. Hannibal implies a North African leader, as does the blue turban of quatrain 9:73. Lyon, France's second largest city, is not benefiting from its new rank as France's largest city, for the destruction of Paris is part of the war that troubles all of France.

Quatrain 10:31

The Holy Empire will come into Germany,
Ishmaelites will find open places:
Asses will also want Carmania,
The supporters by earth are covered.

Basic Interpretation: Even mighty Germany falls prey to the growing Islamic fundamentalist empire.

Detailed Interpretation: The Holy Roman Empire (HRE) was a union comprised mostly of Germanic states. If Nostradamus meant the HRE, the first line would make no sense. But if another religious empire—that of Islam— were meant instead, then the quatrain does make sense.

Especially with the mention of Ishmaelites, the descendants of Ishmael, the son of Abraham that Arabs claim descent from. Arabs may find Germany open to them. That does not necessarily mean Germany will be an ally to them. There might just be many collaborators. Germany's millions of Turkish immigrants may cause a problem similar to France's Algerian immigrants.

The asses will also want Carmania, an ancient province on the Persian Gulf. Perhaps Saddam Hussein's world war casualties make the Iraqi people start to question him. Iraq stands to gain no territory from its enemies as it borders no Christian land. But Hussein could incorporate disputed lands Iraq fought Iran for in the 1980s, although he would be an ass to make enemies of other Muslims such as Iranians or Kuwaitis in the middle of World War III. In any case, Arabs come into Germany, and some Germans apparently support the invaders before being killed and buried. It is hard to blame Germans for collaborating with the occupying armies of Islam. The Muslims may appear to be at the brink of victory. Their Chinese allies may have conquered Asia; Nostradamus is too focused on his French homeland to make many references outside Europe and the Mediterranean. The war could appear lost in Europe and around the world, and many Christians might be more focused on avoiding pointless casualties than on victory at any cost.

Quatrain 9:94

Weak galleys will be joined together,
False enemies, the strongest shall be fortified:
Weak assailed Bratislava trembles,
Lubeck and Meissen will take the barbarian
  side.

Basic Interpretation: Muslim armies fight along a front through Germany and central Europe.

Detailed Interpretation: Weak galleys joined together may refer to many relatively weak forces, perhaps the small nations of Eastern Europe fight the Muslims more vigorously than the mighty French and Germans. Small nations like Serbia and Croatia, former enemies—but now false enemies—because they will be allies against the Muslims, could put up the strongest defense because they have been toughened by their years of fighting and anger over the bombing of Belgrade. In quatrain 10:62 Nostradamus specifically mentions Serbia, Hungary, and Slavonia against a Byzantine chief and the Arabs. He also wrote that Hungary will help Serbia.

Historically, Russia has helped the Serbs defend themselves from attack because the Russians feel a bond to their fellow Slavs. They tried to help in 1914, 1944, and 1999, and may secretly help them fortify their defenses again in World War III. False enemies may also refer to the dubious nature of Russian interests at the start of World War III. At first Russia will try to stay out of the war and let other nations wear themselves out.

Russian leaders may even talk of the Muslims and Chinese as allies in order to buy them time, much like the phony alliance Russia had with Germany from 1939–1941. But Russians know that they have a lot of territory to lose along their southern and eastern borders if Sino-Islamic alliance comes to dominate the world. Russians will view them as potential enemies, and it will make sense for Russians to aid Serbs in order to slow down the advance of their eventual enemies. Even though the Russian media may portray the defenders of Western Europe as enemies, they will really be false enemies (and eventually allies).

It would also make sense for Russia to take over as much territory as possible before they enter the world war against the alliance of Muslims and Chinese. Just as they tried to conquer a protective buffer region in Eastern Europe at the start of World War II, the Russians will probably try to keep their new future enemies at a safer distance. Poland was partitioned with Germany in 1939, and Russia may attempt the same thing in Eastern Europe again, both to rule it themselves and to prevent Muslim rule. They may legitimately see themselves as protectors coming in to prevent an Islamic invasion, but nations that have suffered greatly under past Russian domination may question which invader is worse. Bratislava is the capital of Slovakia (which was known as Pressburg in Nostradamus' time—kudos to him for foreseeing the change in name), and as one of many weak nations in central Europe it trembles between the two advancing forces. Nostradamus indicates in another quatrain that Poland may prefer to ally with the Arabs before they allow the protection of the Russian army back in. Lubeck and Meissen are small cities in Germany, one northwest and one south of Berlin. East Germany also suffered under Soviet occupation, and they will choose defection to the Islamic side as well.

Quatrain 5:73

The Church of God will be persecuted,
And the holy Temples will be spoiled,
The child will put his mother out with only
*   her shirt,*
Arabs will be allied with the Poles.

Basic Interpretation: In a war against Christianity, Poland will ally with the Arabs.

Detailed Interpretation: Perhaps Poland is the child and the Catholic Church is the mother that is so poorly treated. At first it seems strange that any Christian nation would take the Arab side, but Poland has suffered so much at the hands of its Russian neighbors that the Poles just might join the Muslim's side if Christian Europe's cause seems to be lost, especially if the Poles were hoping that the only major neutral nation, Russia, would eventually enter the war and save Christianity— only to see Russia invading Eastern Europe and weakened by internal conflicts or civil war.

Quatrain 4:32

*In the places and times of flesh to fish giving
way,*
*The communal law will be made in
opposition:*
*It will hold strongly the old ones, then
removed from the midst,*
*The Loving of Everything in Common put
far behind.*

Basic Interpretation: Problems in Russia as old-line communists attempt a coup in the spring.

Detailed Interpretation: During the observance of Lent, when fish is eaten instead of meat, there may be a failed attempt to seize power by former communists. The opposition will not have the support of young people who enjoy the current political freedom, but they would have the support of old conservatives yearning for the good old days when they got paid to work and could afford food. The main issue leading to a coup might be that the invasion of Eastern Europe is costly and disagreed upon. The Russian people will feel that Russia is betraying its Christian brothers. If this betrayal leads Poland to side with the Muslims just to hold off a Russian invasion, then the move into Europe will be extremely unpopular. Those in power will be unable to explain the true political reasons of buying time for the eventual war with Russia's true enemies—because the truth would anger the aggressors with whom Russia hopes to avoid war. But the old guard communists will not succeed, and the days of communism will finally be in Russia's past.

Paragraph 27 of the letter to King Henry II:

> *Provinces which will have deserted their old ways to be delivered will be captivated still more. Faith lost in their perfect religion, they will be secretly displeased with their liberty. They commence to stamp out their leftist party and return to the right, only to return to the right. Holiness, for a long time beaten down, will be replaced in accordance with the earliest writings.*

Support for the coup is widespread and complicated. Formerly communist areas will suffer through a slow transition to a market economy. The lack of clear and immediate improvements will make many view the communist era as the good old days. The Russian people react to the tough economic conditions under their reform leaders by supporting former communist officials. Faith lost in Western ways, they will go back and forth between reformers and communists. Religion, once forbidden in Russia, will come back into society as faith in government is lost. These conditions of disunity undermine the support of the government during the war and help lead to civil war and invasion.

Quatrain 8:85

Between Bayonne and Saint Jean-de-Luz
Will be placed the promontory she who
promoted Mars:
For the Hanix of Aquilon Nanar removes
light,
Then suffocated in bed without assistance.

Basic Interpretation: The Iraqi leader will be executed for his failures in France and his invasion of Russia.

Detailed Interpretation: The front line of war—the promontory of Mars—will come to southern France between Bayonne and St. Jean-de-Luz. She who promoted war is probably the whore of Babylon that Nostradamus mentions elsewhere in his prophecies. Edgar Leoni's best guess for Hanix is the Greek word *aniketos*, or in English, "unconquerables."[35] For Nanar he points out the Latin word *nonaria*—a prostitute. Another reference to the whore of Babylon, a reference to Iraq. Aquilon, land of the north wind, is Russia, as Nostradamus makes clear in quatrain 2:68. The enemy leader attacks Russia and removes its light—its hope—for a while.

Things will look very bleak for Russia. In an attempt to delay attacks by Islamic and Chinese forces, they will have moved into Eastern Europe as protectors. This backfires completely, leading to Germans and Poles

---

35 Leoni, ibid., p. 375.

giving up on the cause of Christianity and fighting Russia instead. A coup or even a civil war begins in Russia. This weakens Russia, but takes pressure off the Muslim armies, who become so sure of victory that they attack Russia. The war seems almost over, European nations are switching sides in Christianity's death throes, and the Chinese and Muslim nations want to claim their territorial prizes before the war is over. The easiest territory to claim is just over the border in Russia, where Turkey and Iran and China and other nations can annex adjacent territory.

But the decision to invade Russia is unwise; Russia quickly unifies and proves unconquerable. Poles and Germans reassess the threats to their people and quickly divert their armies to help the Russians and fight the Muslims. (Remember the false enemies mentioned earlier.) The Iraqi leader responsible for the risky and foolish invasion of Russia that could snatch victory from their grasp must be punished. It will be the Iraqi, probably Saddam Hussein, who is suffocated by his own people, without Christian help. This would lead to the rise of the third and final antichrist.

Quatrain 2:91

At sunrise a great fire one will see,
Noise and light towards Aquilon extending:
Within the circle death and cries one will hear,
Through steel, fire, famine, death awaiting
    them.

Poles in the west, Muslims in the south, and Chinese in the east fight Aquilon—Russia—during its brief civil war. On some fronts the Muslim and Chinese aggressors might advance hundreds or even thousands of miles toward the heartland of Russia, but no one approaches Moscow, and it is soon clear that the invasion of Russia was a bad idea. "Death within the circle" only applies to giant modern explosions, as prior wars relied on guns that killed in a linear path. War and death for all involved.

Paragraph 48 of the letter to King Henry II:

> *This will be near the seventh millennary,*
> *when the sanctuary of Jesus Christ will no*
> *longer be tread on.*

Near the year 2000 there are no longer any Soviet troops forcing atheism on Poland or even Russia itself atheist (infidel) government, post-Soviet Russia is a Christian nation again. Edgar Cayce said that Russia would be the savior of Christianity in World War III,[36] and Nostradamus agrees. In the twenty-first century

---

36 Edgar Cayce's predictions were made while in a sleeplike trance and the same quotations can be found in many books under their code numbers. Quotation #3976-10 was made in 1932: "On Russia's religious development will come the greater hope of the world. Then that one or group that is the closer in its relationship [with Russia] may fare better in gradual changes and final settlement of conditions as to the rule of the world." In 1944 he restated "out of Russia comes again the hope of the world" (Quotation #3976-29). Cayce also said that China "will be one day the cradle of Christianity as applied in the lives of men" (reading 3976-29).

Russia is a protector of the Christian Church. In paragraph 54 Nostradamus writes:

> . . . *the third King of Aquilon, hearing the lament of the people of his principal title, will raise a very great army and, defying the tradition of his great-grandfathers, will put almost everything back in it's proper place, and the great Vicar of the hood will be put back in his former state. But desolated, and then abandoned by all, and turning to find the Holy of Holies destroyed by paganism. . .*
>
> .

Eventually the Russian leader, the king of Aquilon, will organize Russia against the invaders. At war first with Poles and other Eastern European nations that fought off previous Soviet domination, then at war with virtually every nation they border, Russia will seem abandoned by all, but they will eventually ally with Christian Europe and defy the atheist traditions of their communist founders three generations earlier. Russians will fight to save the Christian Church, although they do so late in the war, changing their policy only after the destruction of the Holy of Holies (Rome and/ or Israel) by pagans (Muslims).

♦   ♦   ♦

10

The Tide Turns

When Russia finally joins the Christian alliance and survives the initial attacks on it, the end is near for the aggressors.

Paragraph 38 of the letter to King Henry II:

> *Then the Lords, two in number, of Aquilon,*
> *will be victorious over the Easterners, and*
> *so great a noise and bellicose tumult will*
> *they make that all the East will tremble in*
> *terror of these brothers, yet not brothers,*
> *Aquilonaires.*

Civil war or not, the opposing Russian leaders defend their homeland fiercely, and win an important battle.

Quatrain 3:95

The law Moroccan is observed to decay,
After another much more seductive:

> *Boristhenes is the first to come to give way:*
> *By gifts and tongue another more*
> *   attractive.*

Basic interpretation: The Islamic armies will suffer their first major setback in Ukraine.

Detailed interpretation: This quatrain has often been interpreted very differently. Nostradamus used the word *Morique,* which means "of Morocco," but many authors change this to Moorish, which also means of the Moors of Morocco—then they change Moor to More, and say that Nostradamus meant Sir Thomas More and his famous book, *Utopia.* They claim Nostradamus means communism when he refers to More's utopian society. I think it's a stretch to take the French word for Moroccan and get communism out of it, but one author even does this with an interpretation of quatrain 4:85, where the following word is *chameau,* and the two words together translate as "Moorish camel." Somehow this writer still sees Sir Thomas More and communism instead of Morocco.

Perhaps others have been tempted to translate Morique this way because *Borystehenes* is Latin for the Dnieper River in central Ukraine. Most twentieth-century Americans wanted to see the fall of communism there, and perhaps these authors chose to give readers what they wanted, but I think Nostradamus foresaw a twenty-first century event: that Moorish law—Islamic military power—will start to break first in Ukraine.

Besides, communism first broke in East Germany, as the Berlin Wall came down long before the Soviet Union disintegrated.

The Russian army will probably suffer massive initial setbacks when first attacked, then aim to hold back the Chinese front along various natural defenses, eventually falling back to the Ural mountains or Volga River if necessary. Their first offensive goal will be to save their allies in Ukraine, who will find Russian liberators much more attractive than Islamic invaders. Ukrainians and Russians allied together may even be the "brothers, yet not brothers" mentioned in the letter to King Henry II.

Quatrain 2:89

One day the two great masters will be friends,
Their great power will be seen augmented:
The new land will be at its height,
To the bloody one the number recounted.

Basic Interpretation: When the superpowers are on the same side, the antichrist is in trouble.

Detailed Interpretation: The cold war has ended and the two superpowers of Russia and America become allies as they do in every world war. Their powers are increased when not held back to keep each other in check. Having started the war weak and unprepared, the new land of America is at its high peak of war production. Recounting the number of the beast at this time is associated with the coming of the antichrist (third time in this case) and the apocalypse.

Quatrain 6:21

*When those of the arctic pole are united
together,
In the East great dread and fear:
Newly elected, supporting the great trembling,
Rhodes, Byzantium with Barbarian blood
stained.*

Basic Interpretation: America and Russia united together in war make a powerful alliance.

Detailed Interpretation: Only six nations are partially in the arctic. Canada, Norway, Sweden, and Finland are not powerful enough to cause terror and fear. Russia and the United States, however, come closest at the Bering Sea in the Arctic, and would present a formidable alliance to fight. Line three may indicate that a newly elected leader will support the war efforts to defend his nation's interests and allies from aggression.

There are two possibilities for the homeland of this newly elected leader. If the leader is American, perhaps Al Gore will stain the Aegean Sea with enemy blood. In quatrain 10:79 Nostradamus indicates that a great Western warlord will hail from "the modern Memphis." This could be an allegory referring to the fact that Egypt's all-powerful pharaohs ruled from Memphis, and the capital of any leader whose powerful nation is at war could be the modern Memphis. In this case Bush or any president from Washington, D.C., could be indicated, but if Memphis, Tennessee, is meant, Gore is from Tennessee. His election in 2004 would fit Nostradamus' timeline of events. It seems odd now to picture Gore, or any current American politician, as a warlord, but few foresaw the wheelchair-bound Roosevelt sending armies around the world before World War II broke out either.

On the other hand, the leader may not be American. Russia is now an election-holding democracy, and the newly elected leader might be the third king of Aquilon whom Nostradamus mentions earlier. Perhaps after the two leaders in the civil war do enough damage to Russia an election replaces them with a great leader truly fit to lead in times of war.

Quatrain 8:77

The antichrists three very soon annihilated,
Seven and twenty years of blood will last
  his war:
The heretics dead, captives exiled,
Blood body human water reddened to hail
  on land.

Basic interpretation: After reigns of twenty-seven years, all three antichrists are finally annihilated.

Detailed interpretation: Once the third embodiment of the antichrist comes to lead the Islamic alliance, the entire world war, the focus of all three leaders, quickly comes to an end. It is hard to imagine two alliances so evenly matched that a world war could last twenty-seven years. It is more likely that we should consider a twenty-seven-year period of conflict between Islamic and Christian nations starting in 1979, when Russia invaded Afghanistan and Iran took American hostages. This may be when the three antichrists first came to power. Osama bin Laden came to Afghanistan right after the Soviets invaded and began his Holy War. Saddam Hussein took over Iraq in 1979 and soon started a war with Iran. If the third embodiment of the antichrist is from North Africa, then perhaps Benjedid Chadli, who was president of Algeria from 1979 to 1992 fits the bill. The Algerian army ousted him in 1992 to prevent an Islamic fundamentalist seizure of power, but he could be restored to power. If all three antichrists came to power when the Holy War began in 1979, then this would allow an ending date of 2006 for World War III, much more likely than a war lasting until 2029. An end to World War III after four years instead of twenty-seven years also makes more sense for line one, as all three antichrists are soon annihilated.

Paragraph 55 of the letter to King Henry II:

> *After that Antichrist will again be the infernal prince, for the last time, all the kingdoms of Christianity will tremble, even those of the infidels, out of the space of twenty-five years.*

Perhaps Nostradamus means that the world has already trembled for twenty-five years under the threat of Islamic holy war by the time this last antichrist comes to power. This would coincide with other quatrains that indicate that the third antichrist comes to power less than twenty-nine years (less than a reign of Saturn) into the Holy War between the two religions, and that at this point Christianity is done quaking, for victory is almost at hand. Quatrain 10:32 indicates that the short duration of the rule of this meanest one lasts only two years, and those time periods add up to the twenty-seven-year war Nostradamus already described.

Quatrain 10:32

The great empire, everyone would have it,
One over the others will come to obtain it:
But of short duration his realm and state
will be,
Two years on the sea will he maintain
himself.

One contender for the top position after the death of the second antichrist will be more vicious than the others in his ruthless pursuit of power to rule the restored Islamic Empire. Of course, he embodies the spirit of the antichrist—who could be more vicious? This ruler lasts two years.

Quatrain 3:99

In the grassy fields of Alleins and of
Vernegues
Of the Luberon mountains near the
Durance,
The conflict will be harsh for both armies,
Mesopotamia will fail in France.

Basic Interpretation: The Iraqi leader's push into Europe fails in southern France.

Detailed Interpretation: Reminiscent of quatrain 8:85, in which the whore of Babylon fails in France, attacks Russia, and is killed for these acts, Iraq this time is referred to through Mesopotamia instead of Babylon. The Muslim advance finally grinds to a halt in France, with a major battle lost in the southeast near the Durance River.

Quatrain 5:74

Of blood Trojan will be born a heart
Germanic
Who will rise to very high power:
He will chase out the foreign Arabic people,
Returning the Church to pristine
preeminence.

The French monarchy was supposedly descended from King Priam of Troy. A French leader with a German zest for battle (or a German of French ancestry) will drive out the Arabs and restore the Church. This is probably a description of the "King of Europe" mentioned elsewhere.

Quatrain 5:68

In the Danube and of the Rhine will come
*   to drink*
The great Camel, not repenting of it:
Tremble those of the Rhone, and more strong
*   those of the Loire,*
And near the Alps the Cock will ruin him.

The camels drinking in the rivers of Austria and Germany describe the Islamic invasion of central Europe. France trembles in its central and southern areas, but the French leader (the Cock) will defeat the Arabian leader (the great Camel) near the Alps, in southeastern France as described in quatrain 3:99.

Quatrain 10:95

Into the Spains will come a very powerful
*   King,*
By sea and land subjugating the South,
This badly beats down the crescent,
Clipping the wings of those of Friday.

Finally, the King of Europe with the Trojan blood and Germanic heart pushes the Muslims out of France and

Spain. Muslims, those with the symbol of the crescent moon on their flags, those who take Friday as their Sabbath, will finally have their wings clipped, their air force defeated. Nostradamus, very proud and patriotic regarding his native France, probably refuses to give credit where credit is due and acknowledge that the great king is from France's medieval nemesis, England. But France and Germany have no monarchies, Britain does, and the Anglo-Saxon stock of England was greatly influenced by France when the Normans conquered England. England, with its Franco-Germanic heritage, will probably be the source of the great king. Will it be William?

Quatrain 9:42

From Barcelona, from Genoa and Venice,
From Sicily pestilence money unified:
Against the barbarian fleet they will take aim,
Barbarian pushed back as far as Tunis.

Basic Interpretation: Europeans push the Muslim invaders back to North Africa sometime after 2002.

Detailed Interpretation: At the time when local currencies have been unified into the Euro, forces from Spain and Italy will purge the western Mediterranean of Muslim ships, driving them back to North Africa.

Quatrain 2:60

The Punic faith in the Orient broken,
Ganges, Jordan, and Rhone, Loire, and Tagus
   will change:
When the mule's hunger is satisfied,
Fleet scattered, blood and bodies will swim.

"The Punic faith in the Orient broken" could mean that the Islamic alliance loses faith in its Chinese allies, or that Islam, the Punic faith, is defeated in the East. Either way, the Islamic military alliance starts to collapse from India to Portugal, through the Middle East and Europe. It seems likely that India would side with the West in a Third World War against China and Islamic nations.[37] The antichrist's bloodlust (mule's hunger) will soon be drowned in the blood of his own people, and his fleet will be destroyed. Quatrain 10:32 had mentioned he would last only for two years on the sea.

Quatrain 5:80

Ogmios will approach great Byzantium,
Chasing out the Barbarian League,

---

37 The mention of the Islamic advantage being lost near the Ganges River indicates India will be at war, though Nostradamus makes no specific mention of India. It should be emphasized that Nostradamus was overly concerned with his French homeland and those nations closest to France. Great nations like America, China, and India are seldom hinted at, not because they have no role in world affairs, but because they are so far from France.

> *Of two laws the heathen one lets go,*
> *Barbarian and freeman in perpetual strife.*

Basic Interpretation: The Western powers will seize Turkey from the Moslem alliance.

Detailed Interpretation: Ogmios was the Celtic version of Hercules. A great hero will approach Turkey and chase out the Islamic alliance. The war continues.

Quatrain 9:43

> *On the point of landing the Crusader army*
> *Will be ambushed by the Ishmaelites,*
> *Struck from all sides by the ship Impetuosity,*
> *Promptly attacked by ten elite galleys.*

The Christian advance is not easy. There are setbacks. In this case the Arabs are ready for the Christian invaders. They have a naval attack plan ready and waiting, with a flagship and some specially armed ships.

Quatrain 3:97

> *New law new land to occupy,*
> *Towards Syria, Judea, and Palestine:*
> *The great barbarian empire to corrode,*
> *Before Phoebe finishes her great cycle.*

Basic Interpretation: Western newcomers occupy the central Middle East.

Detailed Interpretation: A new rule of law, by way of Western military advances, will come to occupy a new land—not merely the reoccupation of Christian lands like Italy or Spain, but new land that has been under Islamic control since long before World War III began. Syria, Israel, and Jordan will be conquered before the moon goddess completes her great cycle. As the next great cycle of the moon does not end until 2080, and Nostradamus is generally more specific than this on timing, perhaps this reference to the moon is not astronomical, but a symbolic reference to Islam. Nostradamus likens Rome and Christianity to the sun, and probably intends the crescent moon for Islam, as depicted on the flags of many Islamic nations. Unlike the first cycles of Islamic expansion, after which Muslims consolidated their new conquests for centuries, the cycle in World War III will be broken by total defeat.

Quatrain 3:31

On the fields of Media, of Arabia, and of
   Armenia
Two great forces thrice will assemble:
Near the bank of the Araxes the host,
Of great Suleiman's land they will fall.

Basic Interpretation: In the Middle East and central Asia three epic battles lead to the defeat of the Islamic and Chinese forces.

Detailed Interpretation: Media is in Iran. Arabia is dominated by Saudi Arabia. Armenia is between Russia, Turkey, and Iran. The Araxes River is in southern Kazakhstan. This area will host three important military campaigns, leading to defeat for the forces of Islam and China. Iraq is in the middle of this region, and if the decisive campaign of World War III is fought there this could be the apocalyptic battle described in Revelations. Suleiman, the Magnificent, ruled the Ottoman Empire at its peak when Nostradamus was alive. In his time the Islamic empire stretched from Austria to Iran. The forces of the twenty-first century Islamic empire will be defeated in the region between Arabia and Kazakhstan.

> ### Quatrain 10:86
>
> *Like a griffin will come the King of Europe,*
> *Accompanied by those of Aquilon:*
> *Of red ones and white ones he will lead a*
> *   great troop,*
> *And they will go against the King of*
> *   Babylon.*

At this point nothing stops the Christian advance. If red ones and white ones are Spaniards and French (who were known respectively for red and white scarves) as Garencieres claims, then the King of Europe will descend upon the Middle East with the weight of the entire alliance behind him. French and Spanish and Russians (and probably others including British and

Americans, unless they are too busy finishing off Chinese forces in Asia), all advance against the Middle Eastern remainder of the dying Islamic Empire.

Quatrain 1:50

Of the aquatic triplicity is born
One who will make Thursday its holiday:
Its fame, praise, rule, and power will grow,
By land and sea to the Orient a tempest.

Basic Interpretation: The United States fights against Asia.

Detailed Interpretation: Of a land surrounded by three bodies of water (perhaps the Atlantic, Pacific, and Caribbean) a nation with a holiday of Thursday will be born. America's Thanksgiving is the only holiday always on a Thursday, and the United States is the most powerful nation which was not yet born at the time of Nostradamus. This nation's power and prestige will grow, and it will be a military problem for the Orient.

At its peak, the Islamic advance pushes into France and Germany. Poland gives up and joins the Muslims' alliance in order to keep the Russians at bay. Parts of Germany also give up on the cause of Christianity. Russia falls prey to civil war and invasion, and all seems lost for Europe. Then Russia starts to fight back with a vengeance, and this turns the tide in Europe. The European leader pushes the Muslims back out and chases their forces home. Their front collapses from Portugal to

India. American military might, possibly held back in reserve to counter potential Chinese or Russian attacks, is also brought to bear completely once Russia and China are at war. Although decimated by weapons that cause floods and fires and plagues, Europe and Christianity finally emerge victorious. After this Nostradamus concludes his letter to King Henry II with the assurance that after final Christian victory God will bring another golden age and a thousand years of peace.

Quatrain 10:75

Long awaited he will never return,
Within Europe, in Asia he appears:
One of the league issued from the great
  Hermes,
And over the kings of the Orient he
  increases.

The Christian messiah returns not in Europe but in the Middle East. Hermes, the Greek god of wisdom, may indicate that he comes from the ancient Greek area of Asia Minor, which used to be called Asia. Christianity spreads throughout the East.[38]

The religious tone of the war will probably revive Christianity as even nonreligious Westerners will identify with Christian culture over that of their Islamic enemies. The end of the war will also present a unique

---

38 Edgar Cayce also said that China "will be one day the cradle of Christianity as applied in the lives of men" (Reading 3976–29).

settlement issue for what is now Israel if the Muslims perpetrate a second holocaust on the Jews in World War III. The west will not allow Muslims to keep the land as if they won the war, and the Israelis will have been exterminated, along with the Jews that were in Muslim-occupied Europe. Jews who are comfortably assimilated in America probably will not want to leave the United States to go to the old world that repeatedly exterminates Jews. Israel may be repopulated by Christian fundamentalists, and one of their main goals may be to eradicate the culture of violence in the Middle East and replace it with the most peaceful teachings of Christianity.

Quatrain 10:74

The year of the great seventh number accomplished,
It will appear at the time of the games of Sacrifice:
Not far removed from the great millennial age,
When the buried will go out from their tombs.

After the seventh millennium has begun, not long after the year 2000, during a year of the Olympic games, Judgment Day will come.

♦ ♦ ♦

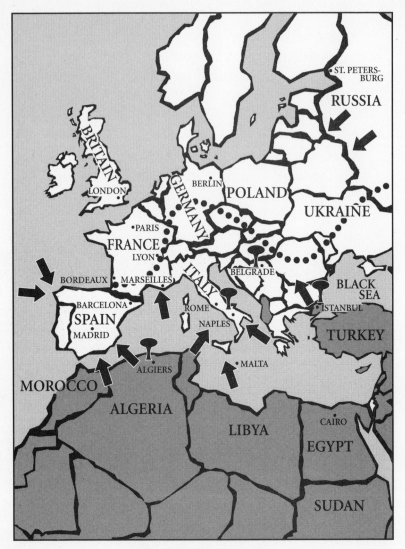

The First Stages of WWIII
Darkened areas are predominantly Islamic countries or areas (including even western China). The mushroom symbol marks four cities that may suffer nuclear destruction.

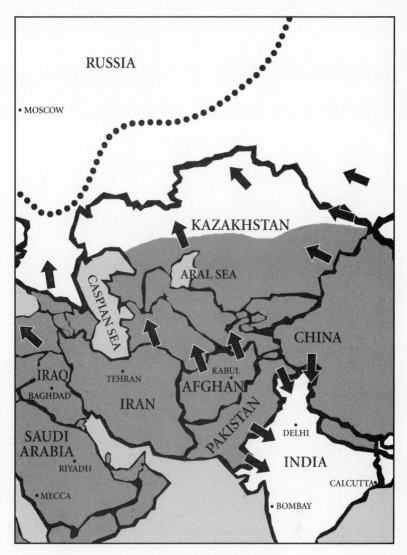

The Second Stages of WWIII
Arrows indicate miltary offensives, and the dotted line indicates the possible furthest advance of the Islamic and Chinese invaders.

11

Nostradamus' Focus in Perspective

There are many topics that Nostradamus barely mentions. In a thousand predictions he mentions America once and alludes to it only two more times. China is alluded to once, as is India. Japan is never mentioned. This is not because these great nations have small roles in history—it is because Nostradamus is French. In theory a Hawaiian prophet might have foreseen World War II and never mentioned Germany in his descriptions; likewise Nostradamus never mentioned Pearl Harbor. The same goes for his description of World War III. Nostradamus focused on his own part of the world; the things he understood best. He also alluded to plagues many times, including paragraph 33 of the letter to King Henry II, in which a plague wipes out "more than two thirds of the world," just as the Bible states in Revelation. In quatrain 5:90 Nostradamus mentions a "plague through false dust," but only describes its long lasting effects in Greece. It sounds like the anthrax already used to contaminate letters in America, but if Nostradamus literally *saw* the future, then perhaps microscopic spores were beyond the focus of his eyes or his understanding. He mentions plague often, the effects of which can be seen clearly, but if manmade biological warfare occurs he leaves the fine details of this apocalypse to our imaginations. The same goes for whether the return of Christ and Judgment Day merely mean that most of the world has died and Christian spirituality will grow throughout the world—or whether Nostradamus meant these events literally.

Of course, most of what he wrote is left up to the imagination. If Nostradamus saw the future and described it too clearly, we would have the paradox of people knowing history and altering it. According to quatrains 1:1 and 1:2, Nostradamus was limited by what he could see in the reflection of a candle flame on the surface of water held in a brass container. As he described the experience to King Henry II in paragraph 12: "It is like seeing in a burning mirror, with cloudy vision."

And as already mentioned earlier, no matter how clearly he could see or understand future events, Nostradamus was also limited in the clarity allowed to his descriptions, both to prevent the paradox of knowing and altering the future, and because the leaders of Church and state would have burned him as a warlock if they were too displeased with his predictions.

With these constraints in mind, consider the prophecies discussed in the next chapter. Although they seem accurate, they are not immediately clear or readily understood. They require lengthy historical explanations, and were therefore placed near the end of this book.

♦ ♦ ♦

12

The Letter to King Henry II

Unlike Nostradamus' quatrains, which are not in chronological order, much of his letter to Henry II is. Many paragraphs contain a highly symbolic but amazingly accurate description of twentieth-century history.

In paragraph 13 Nostradamus says:

> *For God will take notice of the long barrenness of the great dame, who will then conceive two principal children. But she will be in danger, and the female to whom she will have given birth will also, because of the temerity of the age, be in danger of death in the eighteen, and will be unable to live beyond the thirty-six. She will leave three males and one female, and of these two will not have had the same father.*

Democracy is the great dame, Lady Liberty. By the early twentieth century she had been barren for a long time, after bearing the United States in 1776 and France in 1792. World War I would cause the fall of several monarchies; democracy was spread beyond its confines of Britain, America, and France. The wave of democracy in eastern and central Europe is the generation of children of democracy, of which there are two principal offspring.

The first monarch to fall from power was the Russian czar, in late 1917. The people took him prisoner and started forming a democratic type of government. In 1918 (the eighteenth year of the century) the czar was executed, but the new Russian government was in danger, as was the rest of the democratic world, the great dame. The older democracies of Britain, France, and the United States were in danger of losing World War I, and the Russian government was overthrown by Bolshevik communists. Thus, the daughter democracy of Russia died in that eighteenth year, 1918, while the great dame herself, democracy in general, had merely been in danger. The Western Allies won the war and their democratic governments survived. The enemy monarchies were overthrown and replaced with democracies. German democracy followed the removal of Kaiser Wilhelm II in 1918 and Germany, still to be one of the greatest powers in Europe, is the other principal child mentioned in the first sentence. The Austro-Hungarian monarchy also fell and Austria had a democracy.

Political change did not end with the end of the war, however. Benito Mussolini, who was rather moderate initially, seized power from King Victor Emmanuel III in Italy in 1922. The Spanish rulers, King Alfonso XIII, and the dictator who really controlled the nation, General Miguel Primo de Rivera, were overthrown by a socialist assembly in 1931. Numerous offspring were suddenly born by democracy, the great dame that had been barren for so long.

But they did not last. Within a few years after taking charge, Mussolini amassed all the power he could and turned Italy into a fascist dictatorship. In 1933 Adolf Hitler disposed of German democracy, the Weimar Republic, and Germany became a Nazi dictatorship. In 1933 Austrian democracy was replaced by the authoritarian (and pro-Nazi) regimes of Dollfuss and then Schuschnigg. In 1936 civil war broke out in Spain, and the democracy of the republican government there was soon replaced with the fascist dictatorship of Francisco Franco. Russia had already been under Joseph Stalin's communist dictatorship for years. Thus all the new democracies born in the twentieth century in Europe were "unable to live beyond the 36," the thirty-sixth year of the century of democracy. Yet "she will leave three males and one female," with all different fathers. Since Germany absorbed the German-speaking nation of Austria, only four children remained: three fascist fatherlands (Germany, Italy, and Spain) and one communist motherland (Russia). Three males and one female, each with a different founder (father) responsible for their governments' existence: Hitler, Mussolini, Franco, and Stalin.

Paragraphs 14–16 are also fairly accurate, but lengthy to explain. (By all means, look them up. This book should not be your only source of information on Nostradamus; it is just one man's opinion.) In paragraph 17, Nostradamus writes:

> *The daughter will be given for the conservation of the Christian Church. Her lord will fall into the pagan sect of the new infidels. Of her two children, one will be faithful to the Catholic Church, the other an infidel.*

The Soviet Union is the daughter of Mother Russia, and her leadership did fall into the hands of atheistic, communist infidels. Although religion was outlawed in Soviet Russia, Nostradamus later indicates that not only will Christianity be revived in Russia (which has already happened), but that one day Russia will save European Christianity from non-Christians. Of communism's two children, one will be Christian, and one an infidel. Russia and China? Or the Moscow-spawned Latin American bloc of Catholic communists, as opposed to the Beijing-spawned bloc of communists in Asia?

Paragraph 18 reverts back to World War II:

*The unfaithful son, who, to his great
confusion and later repentance, will want
to ruin her, will have three regions at
extreme distances, namely, the Roman, the
German, and the Spanish, which will set up
diverse sects by military force. He will leave
behind the 50th to the 52nd degree of
latitude.*

The male fascist fatherland nations of Italy, Germany, and Spain (which are clearly named and which became fascist in that order) will try to destroy Russia. Although Spain was officially neutral in World War II, tens of thousands of Spanish volunteers did join the German army to fight Russia. The three fascist nations had military dictatorships. Hitler's primary goal in late 1940 was to defeat England (London is at 51.5 degrees north) but he reluctantly concluded that Germany could not storm the island directly, and that the British would not surrender because they had a reasonable hope that Russia, growing ever stronger as Germany weakened itself in a long war, would eventually join them. Hitler abandoned the plans to invade England directly and focused on the indirect route of defeating its potential Russian ally.

Paragraph 19:

And all will render the homage of ancient
religions of the region of Europe north of the
48th parallel. The latter will have trembled
first in vain timidity but then the regions to
its west, south, and east will tremble. But the
nature of their power is such that what has
been made by concord and union will prove
insuperable by warlike conquests.

The Nazis did like the myth and mysticism of ancient Scandinavia. Denmark and Norway, the western half of Scandinavia, fell in April 1940. May and June saw the Germans change their northern focus to a western one, as the Low Countries, France, and Britain were attacked. Later fighting took place in Greece and North Africa to the south, and eventually to the Russian front in the east. Russia did not fall because the nations of the allies were strong in spirit and united in purpose, and they were unions even in name, the United States, the United Kingdom, and the Union of Soviet Socialist Republics. They proved unconquerable.

Paragraph 20:

They will be equal in nature, but very
different in faith.

The main victors became the new superpowers, of roughly equal strength, but very different ideologies:

democracy and capitalism and religion on one side, dictatorship and communism and atheism on the other.

Paragraph 21 jumps ahead several decades again:

> *After this the sterile dame, of greater power than the second, will be received by two peoples. First, by them made obstinate by the one-time masters of the universe. Second, by the masters themselves.*

Democracy and capitalism proved to be more economically feasible and of greater power than communism. After the period referred to in paragraph 20 when the ideologically different superpowers oppose each other, democracy overpowers and replaces the totalitarian governments in two nations. First, for the Germans who were defeated by their Russian masters, East Germany joining the West German democracy in 1990; second by the Russians themselves after the fall of the Soviet government in 1991.

In paragraph 25, Nostradamus backtracks to 1991 again, as already mentioned, with the Soviet Union lasting seventy-three years and seven months. The role of Pope John Paul II is described in paragraph 26, and the disunity in Russia leading to a coup attempt in paragraph 27.

Paragraphs 28 to 33 ramble on about the antichrist, persecution of the Church, and trouble caused by Easterners. In 33, Nostradamus says that a plague will wipe out two-thirds of the world, and begins to write about specific places like Rome and the southern French port of Marseilles, places of great activity at the time of the world conflict's beginning. Paragraph 34 describes the Muslim invasion of Spain.

In paragraph 36, World War III ends and Nostra-damus says nothing of history after that, except that there is a long reign of peace and the world finally ends in 3797.

♦　♦　♦

13

Nothing for Certain

This entire book is highly speculative. If correct, future readers may wonder why no one took the warnings seriously. If incorrect, future readers will mock me for having believed such things. Nostradamus mocks future interpreters. He warned in quatrain 6:100's incantation against inept critics:

> *Let those who read these verses consider them profoundly, Let the profane, vulgar and ignorant keep away, far away all astrologers, blockheads, and Barbarians.*

Did he write this because the prophecies are just a big joke? Or because they address matters that should be taken very seriously?

Did Nostradamus really foresee World War III starting in 2002? This question presupposes that it is possible for a human being to have such visions of the future, and that Nostradamus had the psychic gift necessary to foresee future events. Some would argue that such alleged supernatural powers are always a hoax, and that Nostradamus' prophecies in particular are uselessly vague. Others point out that prophecies have always been clear in hindsight, but are vague beforehand to avoid a paradox: that a clearly worded prediction of any important event would be acted upon and made false.

For example, assume that a psychic foresees the assassination of a president. If the prediction is publicized and believed, would that president ignore the warnings? If Kennedy had read a clearly detailed prophecy of his own coming assassination and had taken it seriously, he would have avoided public appearances on November 22, 1963. He would have avoided traveling in a motorcade in Dallas, and he would have had Lee Harvey Oswald held in custody that day. Such actions, however, would negate the event that had been foreseen, and this would cause a paradox that the universe does not allow. If the future was truly seen, then the timeline of events is set and cannot be changed; therefore events that would cause its change cannot happen. Prophecies will never be made that are so clear that the correct interpretation will be taken seriously by those in power to make history.

Nostradamus addresses these problems repeatedly in a letter to his son Caesar. He describes the future he foresees as fixed and unchangeable, that "past, present,

---

39 Leoni, ibid., p. 127, citing paragraph 17 of Nostradamus' letter to his son Caesar, written in 1555.

and future become one eternity."[39] The future cannot be changed any more than the past. Therefore even though Nostradamus, who was not inclined to try to alter the future, could have accurately dated every prophecy, "all had to be written under a nebulous figure."[40] He understood that ". . . if I come to disclose what will happen in the future, the leaders of the above kingdoms. . . ."[41] would try to change their policies. Such a paradox cannot occur. Nostradamus claimed divine inspiration, but this is not meant for everyone. He only wants us to understand the course of events after the fact: "When it is time for the removal of ignorance, the event will be cleared up more."[42]

Admittedly, this argument is rather convenient for those of us who promote the idea that the future can be foreseen. It is an excuse for the vagueness of prophecy, and many intelligent people will not take such things seriously without the kind of empirical evidence that will never come. For those who understand these limitations, and have a more open mind regarding the idea that prophecy is possible, Nostradamus has done a remarkable job of wording his prophecies. None are crystal clear to the point where national leaders are basing policy on them, but many are clear enough successes that those with an open mind can see the link between certain prophecies and historical events.

---

40 Ibid., paragraph 6.

41 Ibid., paragraph 5.

42 Ibid., paragraph 33.

Appendix

About Nostradamus

Michel de Nostradamus was born in 1503 to a prominent family of doctors and astrologers in southern France. Educated by both grandfathers and eventually at the University of Montpelier, Nostradamus was granted a doctor's license in 1525. Although he treated victims of the Black Plague with greater success than most doctors, the unusual medicines he created concerned his peers, and he was not allowed to teach his own methods when given a faculty position in 1529. The restrictions of his profession and the despair of failing to save his own family from the plague eventually shifted his focus back to astrology and the occult. By 1550 he published his first almanac of prophecies, and he soon achieved greater fame for his mysterious predictions of future events than he ever had for healing the sick.

Unfortunately, his predictions often seem meaningless to readers, especially to those unfamiliar with European history.

Nostradamus had many reasons to make his writings difficult to understand, notably the Inquisition. His Jewish ancestors had fled the Spanish Inquisition and settled in the more tolerant kingdom of Provence in southern France, but times had changed. Even though the family had converted to Christianity, such converts were often harassed as Jews. France was in a state of political and religious turmoil, and Nostradamus knew that if he annoyed anyone with power in the government or the Church, they would hold his background against him as well. It was unwise for anyone to claim the ability to see the future if they wished to avoid harassment from the Inquisition. In the 1550s the Catholic Church was persecuting people for Protestant beliefs; a minor heresy when compared to the use of magical powers bestowed by the devil. Nostradamus could have been burned at the stake for predicting the future, especially if his prophecies foretold unpleasant events for the Church—which they do. In paragraph six of the Preface to his *Centuries,* Nostradamus explained to his son that he was forced to write "by dark and cryptic sentences. . . . In a manner that would not upset their fragile sentiments."

Nostradamus also foretells unpleasant events in the future of the French monarchy, and if the king felt that Nostradamus had insulted his legacy he could have had the prophet put to death as well. To make sure that no one in power would dislike what he said, Nostradamus made his writing extremely difficult for them to understand. He rearranged the letters in some words, and used other words and names from mythology that most people would not recognize. He even used words from foreign languages such as Hebrew, Greek, and Latin. In addition he usually did not give the time a prophecy would be fulfilled the easy way—by telling us the year—he usually mentioned an astronomical conjunction, and only an astronomer could figure out when the planets he mentioned would be in that exact arrangement in the sky. Given such constraints, he accomplished an amazing feat.

◆   ◆   ◆

Selected Bibliography

Garencieres, Theophilus. *The True Prophecies or Prognostications of Michael Nostradamus.* London: Thomas Ratcliffe and Nathaniel Thompson, 1672.

Leoni, Edgar. *Nostradamus and his Prophecies.* New York: Bell Publishing, 1982.

Nostradamus, Michel. *Les Vrayes Centuries et Propheties de Maistre Michel Nostradamus.* Cologne: Jean Volcker, 1689.

Randi, James. *The Mask of Nostradamus.* New York: Charles Scribner's Sons, 1990.

Index

☽ REACH FOR THE MOON

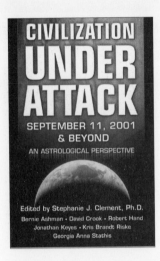

Civilization
Under Attack

Edited by
Stephanie J. Clement, Ph.D.

September 11, 2001 & Beyond
Making sense of the senseless

This was the day our world changed forever. The seven contributors of this book use the wisdom of astrology to bring understanding to an otherwise incomprehensible situation. They consider the indicators of the attack, the historical and political under-pinnings of the new global threat, and the long-range effects of the new war on terrorism.

The information is presented in easy-to-understand language, with copious footnotes, charts, and astro maps for the astrologically inclined.

- Deepen our understanding of the psychology of terrorism
- Provides astrological analysis for key figures including George W. Bush, Dick Cheney, Colin Powell, and Osama bin Laden
- Explores how the United State's astrological chart for July 4, 1776, reflects recent events

0-7387-0247-1, 264 pp., 5³⁄₁₆ x 8, charts and maps $10.95

The Comet of Nostradamus: August 2004—Impact!

R. W. Welch

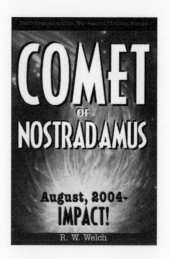

He foresaw the French Revolution and the rise of Napoleon. He perceived World War II 400 years before it happened as well as more recent events, such as the Persian Gulf War and the Reagan and Clinton administrations.

In this book, you will discover what Nostradamus saw for the years following 2000—a giant comet hurling toward Europe, and a great war extending throughout the Mediterranean and beyond.

What's more, scores of previously undeciphered or misapplied quatrains are successfully decoded, making *The Comet of Nostradamus* the most significant advance in Nostradamian interpretation since the work of Le Pelletier in the mid-nineteenth century.

Because the weight we give to Nostradamus' predictions for our times hinges on his accuracy in the past, a large portion of the book analyzes the percentage of Nostradmus' prophecies that qualify as psychic hits.

1-56718-816-8, 336 pp., 6 x 9 $14.95

Predictions for a
New Millennium
Noel Tyl

He predicted the exact dates of the Gulf War and the fall of the Soviet Union. Now Noel Tyl foresees key events, with fifty-eight predictions about the dramatic political, economic, and social changes that will occur between now and the year 2012. *Predictions for a New Millennium* prepares us to see beyond the crisis of the moment to understand world changes strategically. Here are just a few of the momentous events that we will witness as we enter the 21st century: assassination of another U.S. president . . . China abandons communism . . . Saddam Hussein toppled from power . . . Hitler revival in Germany. The new millennium is a pivotal time in our history. How will these events affect the economy, the world powers . . . how will they affect you? The answers are here.

1-56718-737-4, 304 pp., 6 x 9, maps, graphs $14.95

The Pythagorean Tarot
John Opsopaus,
Illustrations by Rho

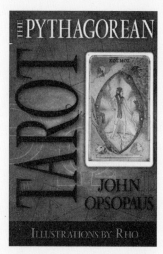

If Pythagoras had designed a tarot deck. . .

To many of us, Pythagoras was the ancient Greek mathematician who developed the theorem for right triangles. But he was also a philosopher and a magician—and, some would argue, the founder of the entire Western occult tradition.

Most ways of understanding the Tarot owe a major debt to Pythagoras. Finally, a deck has been created that focuses on Pythagorean numerology. The tarot contains the usual set of 22 Major Arcana and 56 Minor Arcana cards, but with an order based on an older system. The symbolism and meanings follow the traditions of ancient Greek Pagan spirituality and philosophy, with Greek lettering, Greek and Roman deities, and a Latin motto. In addition, the author has devised two different systems using dice for selecting individual Arcana.

- Rooted in ancient Greek Paganism and esoteric doctrine
- Based on the oldest historical records
- Illuminates deep patterns in mythology, the archetypes, Paganism, alchemy, and numerology

1-56718-449-9 **$39.95 U.S.**

Boxed kit: 78-card deck and 6 x 9, 480-pp. illustrated guidebook

Out of Time and Space: Amazing Accounts that Challenge Our View of Human History

Compiled by Terry O'Neill

I held my hand out of the wagon window and caught four fat, brown little toads . . . I had heard of fish and frogs falling from the clouds, but I had never heard of a fall of toads . . .

— "Does it Rain Toads?"

Explore fascinating mysteries of history, archaeology, and the paranormal with this collection of amazing reports published only in the pages of FATE magazine. The writers of these fascinating articles follow the footsteps of Indiana Jones, seeking the lost and trying to solve the mysteries of the oddly found. Thirty original articles from the best of FATE over the past forty years feature tales of lost cities, strange falls from the sky, extraordinary creatures, and misplaced artifacts that call into question our entire view of human history.

Despite studies by historians and scientists from many fields, these events and objects from out of time and place remain unexplained. Readers can't resist being enthralled by these mysteries and by the efforts to solve them.

1-56718-261-5, 272 pp., 5³⁄₁₆ x 8   **$9.95**